JENSEN HUANG'S
NVIDIA

Processing the Mind of Artificial Intelligence

Daniel D. Lee

★★★★★

Introduction

Overview of Jensen Huang, Nvidia, and their role in the AI industry

Chapter 1: Tracing the Origins: Jensen Huang

Detailed account of Jensen Huang's early life, education, and formative experiences

Exploration of his introduction to technology and computers, and the initial seeds of his interest in this field

Analysis of his higher education journey, focusing on how his studies influenced his vision and future career

Chapter 2: Nvidia: The Birth of a Tech Giant

Detailed history of Nvidia's foundation and early years

Discussion of the initial challenges, achievements, and pivotal developments that shaped Nvidia's trajectory

Chapter 3: Pioneering Innovations: Nvidia's Technological Evolution

Detailed look at Nvidia's technological journey, from graphics processing to AI and data centers

Analysis of strategic shifts and innovations that propelled Nvidia to the forefront of the tech industry

Chapter 4: Powering the Game: Nvidia's Impact on Video Gaming

Detailed exploration of Nvidia's significant role in the video gaming industry

Examination of how Nvidia's GPUs revolutionized computer graphics and gaming experiences

Discussion of Nvidia's gaming-specific products, technologies, and partnerships

Analysis of Nvidia's influence on emerging gaming trends, such as virtual reality and cloud gaming

Insights into how Nvidia's work in gaming continues to intersect with its broader AI initiatives

Chapter 5: Proof of Work: Nvidia and Cryptocurrency Mining

Overview of the role of Nvidia's GPUs in cryptocurrency mining

Examination of how Nvidia's GPUs facilitate the mining of

Chapter 9: The Generative AI Revolution and Nvidia's Pioneering Role

Explanation of generative AI and its potential for transformation in various industries

Exploration of Nvidia's involvement with generative AI, its collaborations with leading AI organizations, and its role in revolutionary technologies like ChatGPT

Chapter 10: Nvidia's Competitive Edge in the AI Chip Industry

Analytical look at Nvidia's position and strengths in the AI chip market

Exploration of the unique capabilities and attributes that give Nvidia a competitive advantage in AI processing

Chapter 11: The Advent of Robotics: Nvidia's Early Contributions

Detailed account of Nvidia's initial foray into the field of robotics

Analysis of the technologies and strategies that have driven Nvidia's success in this arena

Chapter 12: The Future of Robotics: Nvidia's Vision and Innovations

In-depth look at the cutting-edge robotics technologies currently being developed by Nvidia

Expert predictions and analysis of how Nvidia's work in robotics could shape the future of the industry

Chapter 13: The Nvidia Stock Phenomenon

In-depth analysis of Nvidia's stock performance, with exploration of the driving factors behind its growth

Examination of the company's financial prospects, with insights from financial analysts and industry experts

Chapter 14: The Financial Ripple Effect

Detailed discussion of Nvidia's financial success and its wider implications for the tech industry and the economy

Analysis of Jensen Huang's growing wealth and influence, and what this indicates about the state of the tech industry

Chapter 15: The Road Ahead: Nvidia's Future in AI

Analysis of Nvidia's potential future role in the AI industry

Insights into Jensen Huang's vision for the future of AI and Nvidia's place in it

The future implications of these chip advancements and the launch of Eos supercomputer

Nvidia's continued focus on AI development, as seen in its 2023 advancements

The potential influence of Nvidia's advancements in healthcare, automotive, and other sectors

Conclusion

Reflection on Nvidia's journey, its transformative impact on AI, and its influence on the tech industry

Summary of Jensen Huang's visionary leadership and its role in Nvidia's success

Final thoughts on the potential implications and opportunities for Nvidia in the rapidly evolving AI landscape.

Addendum

INTRODUCTION

In the transformative landscape of technology, one name stands out prominently - Jensen Huang, the co-founder and CEO of Nvidia, a company that has redefined the possibilities of artificial intelligence (AI). Nvidia's journey from a manufacturer of graphics processing units (GPUs) to a leader in the AI industry is an extraordinary testament to innovation, resilience, and vision. Huang, a pivotal figure in this journey, has led the company with a unique blend of technological expertise and strategic leadership.

This book, "Jensen Huang's Nvidia: Processing the Mind of Artificial Intelligence," delves into the captivating journey of Nvidia under Huang's leadership. It offers readers an in-depth understanding of the company's evolution, the technological revolutions it has spearheaded, and its defining role in shaping the AI landscape.

The first chapter traces the origins of Jensen Huang, providing a detailed account of his early life, education, and the experiences that sparked his interest in technology. It explores the influence of his higher education on his career trajectory and his vision for Nvidia.

The subsequent chapters delve into the history and growth of Nvidia, the challenges it encountered, and the strategic decisions that have shaped its trajectory. From its roots as a GPU manufacturer to its evolution into an AI and data center pioneer, Nvidia's journey is as fascinating as it is enlightening.

As the narrative unfolds, the book delves deeper into the specifics of AI technology, the role of chips in facilitating AI, and Nvidia's significant contributions to the evolution of AI chips. It explores Nvidia's AI chips, their functionality, and their importance in AI technologies.

Further chapters discuss Nvidia's integral role in the AI boom, the company's competitive edge in the AI chip industry, and the unique attributes that give Nvidia a competitive advantage in AI processing. The narrative also explores the Nvidia stock phenomenon and the implications of Nvidia's financial success on the broader tech industry and economy.

In the concluding chapters, the book provides expert insights into Nvidia's potential future role in the AI industry and the visionary roadmap of Jensen Huang.

This book is more than just a history of a tech company; it's a journey through the mind of a visionary, the heartbeat of a tech giant, and the future of AI. As you delve into these pages, you will witness the transformative power of technology and the limitless potential of human ingenuity. Whether you're a tech enthusiast, a business professional, or someone curious about the future of AI, this book offers valuable insights and perspectives. Welcome to the journey of "Jensen Huang's Nvidia: Processing the Mind of Artificial Intelligence."

Overview of Jensen Huang, Nvidia, and their role in the AI industry

Jensen Huang is an influential figure in the tech industry, known for his role as the co-founder and CEO of Nvidia, a multinational technology company specializing in the design of graphics processing units (GPUs) and artificial intelligence (AI) technology. Born in Taiwan and raised in the United States, Huang's passion for technology and his entrepreneurial spirit led him to co-found Nvidia in 1993, and he has been at the helm ever since. His leadership, vision, and technical acumen have been instrumental in shaping Nvidia into a leading force in the global tech industry.

Nvidia was initially recognized for its role in developing GPUs, which transformed the gaming industry by offering stunningly realistic graphics. However, the company's influence extends far beyond gaming. Nvidia's GPUs have been repurposed for parallel processing, a computational approach that is vital in the realm of AI. By processing large and complex datasets simultaneously, these GPUs accelerate the training of machine learning models, making Nvidia a key player in the AI industry.

Under Huang's guidance, Nvidia has also ventured into the development of AI-specific hardware, such as the Tensor Core GPUs and Nvidia's AI platform, Jetson. These innovations have enabled significant advancements in various fields, including autonomous vehicles, healthcare, and robotics.

Nvidia's role in the AI industry cannot be overstated. Its GPUs power many of the world's supercomputers and are extensively used in deep learning, a subset of AI that aims to mimic the human brain's ability to learn and make decisions. Furthermore, Nvidia's software libraries, such as CUDA and cuDNN, have made it easier for researchers and developers to harness the power of GPUs for AI workloads.

In summary, Jensen Huang's leadership and Nvidia's technological innovations have been integral to the growth and evolution of the AI industry. Their contribution is set to continue into the future, as AI becomes increasingly central to technology and society.

CHAPTER 1: TRACING THE ORIGINS: JENSEN HUANG

Detailed account of Jensen Huang's early life, education, and formative experiences

Jensen Huang was born on February 17, 1963, in Tainan, Taiwan. His family later moved to Oneida, Kentucky, where Huang spent his childhood. From an early age, Huang displayed an affinity for technology and a curiosity about how things work.

In his high school years, Huang nurtured a fascination for mathematics and science, subjects that would later form the foundation of his technological pursuits. His family's move to Oregon further expanded his horizons, exposing him to the vibrant tech scene in the Pacific Northwest.

Upon graduating from Aloha High School in Oregon, Huang enrolled at Oregon State University. His college years were a pivotal period in his life, shaping his career trajectory and seeding his entrepreneurial ambitions. He pursued a degree in Electrical Engineering, a field that allowed him to delve deep into his interest in technology and its applications. His college experience fostered his analytical thinking, problem-solving skills, and understanding of technological principles, which would later become crucial in his role as Nvidia's co-founder and CEO.

Huang's thirst for knowledge didn't stop at undergraduate studies. He furthered his education at Stanford University, where he earned a master's degree in Electrical Engineering. Stanford, known for its strong ties to Silicon Valley and a culture of innovation, had a profound influence on Huang. The environment nurtured his entrepreneurial spirit and exposed him to the fast-paced world of tech startups.

During his time at Stanford, Huang was not only a diligent student but also a visionary dreamer. He spent countless hours discussing potential business ideas with his peers, reflecting on the future of technology, and envisioning how he could contribute to the tech industry.

These early experiences and educational opportunities played a significant role in shaping Huang's perspective on technology and entrepreneurship. They equipped him with the knowledge, skills, and vision that would become instrumental in the foundation and growth of Nvidia.

Jensen Huang's early life and education were not just about the accumulation of knowledge and skills. They were a transformative journey that sparked his passion for technology, nurtured his entrepreneurial spirit, and shaped his vision for a future driven by AI. His story serves as a testament to the power of education, the importance of curiosity, and the transformative potential of technology.

Exploration of his introduction to technology and computers, and the initial seeds of his interest in this field

Jensen Huang's journey into the world of technology began at a young age. Growing up in a time when the digital revolution was just beginning to take hold, Huang's interest in technology was piqued by the emergence of personal computers in the late 1970s and early 1980s.

Huang's early fascination with computers was stimulated by their capacity to solve complex problems and their potential to revolutionize the way we live and work. His introduction to computers came when he first interacted with an Apple II, one of the first successful mass-produced microcomputers. He was captivated by the machine's ability to execute commands and generate outputs based on the user's input. The sense of control and the ability to create and modify digital environments was a revelation to him.

Huang was also deeply interested in the inner workings of these machines. This interest led him to pursue a Bachelor's degree in Electrical Engineering from Oregon State University. During his time at the university, Huang gained a more profound understanding of computer architecture, integrated circuits, and digital logic design. His academic pursuits only further fueled his passion for technology and laid a solid foundation for his future endeavors.

Huang's early professional career also played a role in shaping his interest in the field. Before founding Nvidia, he worked at LSI Logic, a semiconductor company, and Advanced Micro Devices (AMD), a multinational company specializing in computer processors and related technologies. These experiences provided him with valuable industry insights and a deep understanding of the technological needs and trends of the time.

In essence, Huang's introduction to technology and computers was a mix of personal curiosity, academic learning, and professional experience. These factors combined to sow the initial seeds of his interest in this field, ultimately leading him to co-found Nvidia and pioneer innovations in graphics processing and artificial intelligence.

*Analysis of his higher education
journey, focusing on how
his studies influenced his
vision and future career*

Jensen Huang's journey through higher education, especially his time at Stanford University, played a crucial role in molding his future career and the vision he carried into his professional life. As he pursued his master's degree in Electrical Engineering, Huang found himself immersed in an environment that bred innovation and nurtured the spirit of entrepreneurship. Stanford, with its deep connections to Silicon Valley, provided Huang with a unique perspective on the rapid advancement of technology and its potential to transform societies.

Throughout his time at Stanford, Huang was exposed to a variety of cutting-edge technologies and concepts that were set to shape the future of the tech industry. He studied subjects like VLSI design, computer architecture, and artificial intelligence – areas that would later become integral to his work at Nvidia.

One of the defining aspects of Huang's education at Stanford was the culture of innovation and entrepreneurial spirit that permeated the campus. Surrounded by some of the brightest minds in technology, Huang was inspired to think beyond traditional boundaries and envision new possibilities for technology's role in society.

During his studies, Huang often found himself in deep discussions with his peers about the future of technology, potential business ideas, and the rapid evolution of the tech industry. These conversations, combined with the knowledge and skills he was acquiring through his coursework, helped shape Huang's vision for a company that could leverage the power of technology to drive innovation.

Huang's master's thesis, which focused on network interconnect architecture, provided him with a deep understanding of the fundamental building blocks of computing technology. This knowledge would later become crucial in his role as the co-founder of Nvidia, a company known for its innovations in graphics processing and AI technologies.

Furthermore, Stanford's close ties with Silicon Valley provided Huang with numerous opportunities to interact with tech industry leaders, venture capitalists, and innovative startups. These interactions expanded his understanding of the business side of the tech industry, teaching him valuable lessons about building and scaling a successful tech company.

In essence, Jensen Huang's higher education journey was a pivotal period in his life, shaping his vision for Nvidia and equipping him with the skills, knowledge, and insights necessary to lead a tech giant. His time at Stanford not only prepared him for the technological challenges he would face but also instilled in him the entrepreneurial spirit and strategic thinking that have become the hallmarks of his leadership at Nvidia.

CHAPTER 2: NVIDIA: THE BIRTH OF A TECH GIANT

Detailed history of Nvidia's foundation and early years

Nvidia's story began in 1993 when three ambitious and talented computer scientists, Jensen Huang, Chris Malachowsky, and Curtis Priem, co-founded the company. The name "Nvidia" was chosen for its roots in Latin, meaning "envy," a reference to the "envy" of the company's innovative technology and vision.

At its inception, Nvidia was a venture into the uncharted territories of graphics processing. The founders recognized that graphics processing could become a major industry due to the growing demand for better visuals in video games and the advent of Microsoft's Windows operating system, which introduced a graphical user interface that required more advanced graphics capabilities.

The company's first major product, the NV1, was launched in 1995. While the NV1 showcased Nvidia's potential, its market success was limited due to its unconventional design. The NV1 used quadratic texture mapping, a different approach than the traditional triangle-based rendering used in most graphics cards. This made it challenging for game developers to adapt their software to the NV1's unique architecture.

However, Nvidia quickly learned from the experience and shifted its strategy. In 1997, Nvidia released the RIVA 128 (Real-time Interactive Video and Animation accelerator), which was a triangle-based rendering GPU. This product was a significant success, and it established Nvidia as a serious contender in the graphics processing market.

The following year, in 1998, Nvidia introduced the GeForce 256, the first GPU to offload geometry calculations from the CPU, freeing up the CPU for other tasks and dramatically improving graphics performance. This innovation set a new standard in the industry and solidified Nvidia's reputation as a pioneering force in graphics technology.

The early years of Nvidia were characterized by rapid innovation, resilience, and a clear vision of the future. Despite initial setbacks, the founders remained committed to their vision of creating cutting-edge graphics technology. The lessons learned, the challenges overcome, and the achievements made during these foundational years laid the groundwork for Nvidia's future success and its eventual foray into artificial intelligence.

Discussion of the initial challenges, achievements, and pivotal developments that shaped Nvidia's trajectory

When Jensen Huang co-founded Nvidia in 1993 along with Chris Malachowsky and Curtis Priem, the tech landscape was ripe for disruption. They envisioned a company that would revolutionize the way graphics were processed and displayed on computers. However, transforming this vision into reality was no small feat. The initial years of Nvidia were marked by significant challenges, key achievements, and pivotal developments that would shape the company's trajectory.

One of the first challenges Nvidia faced was establishing itself in the competitive landscape of semiconductor companies. At that time, several well-established companies were already dominating the market. Breaking into this industry required not only a superior product but also the ability to convince potential customers of its value. Nvidia's first product, the NV1, was an innovative graphics and audio card, but it didn't achieve the desired commercial success, mostly due to its unconventional design.

Despite the initial setback, Nvidia persevered. The team learned from the NV1's shortcomings and focused their efforts on developing a product that would deliver exceptional graphics processing capabilities. This led to the creation of the RIVA series of graphics processors, which successfully positioned Nvidia as a serious player in the GPU market.

The pivotal moment in Nvidia's history came with the introduction of the GeForce 256 in 1999, the world's first Graphics Processing Unit (GPU). This innovation revolutionized the industry by offloading graphics processing from the

CPU, allowing for more realistic and complex graphics. This development marked a significant achievement for Nvidia and established the company as a leader in graphics processing technology.

Simultaneously, Nvidia had to navigate the business challenges that came with rapid growth. Building partnerships with major computer manufacturers, managing supply chain complexities, and scaling production to meet increasing demand were among the many hurdles the company had to overcome.

One of the critical decisions that shaped Nvidia's trajectory was its strategic focus on research and development. The company invested heavily in R&D, betting on the future of graphics processing and, later, AI technologies. This commitment to innovation allowed Nvidia to stay ahead of the curve and continually deliver groundbreaking products.

The early years of Nvidia were a testament to the company's resilience and commitment to innovation. The challenges it faced forged its character, the achievements validated its vision, and the strategic decisions set the course for its future. From its inception, Nvidia demonstrated the audacity to dream big, the tenacity to overcome obstacles, and the foresight to invest in the future - qualities that continue to drive its success in the ever-evolving landscape of technology.

CHAPTER 3: PIONEERING INNOVATIONS: NVIDIA'S TECHNOLOGICAL EVOLUTION

Detailed look at Nvidia's technological journey, from graphics processing to AI and data centers

Nvidia's technological journey has been marked by continuous innovation and an uncanny ability to foresee and respond to shifts in the tech industry. Starting as a graphics processing company, Nvidia evolved to become a central player in the realms of artificial intelligence (AI) and data centers.

The company's early years were focused primarily on developing graphics processing units (GPUs). Nvidia's GPUs, starting with the RIVA series and later the GeForce line, brought significant advancements to the video gaming industry by providing higher quality graphics and more efficient processing. The GeForce 256, launched in 1998, was particularly groundbreaking as it was the first GPU to offload geometry calculations from the CPU, improving overall computer performance.

While Nvidia continued to enhance its GPUs and dominate the gaming market, a paradigm shift occurred when researchers realized that the parallel computing capabilities of these GPUs could be harnessed for general-purpose computing tasks, such as those required by AI algorithms. This led to the development of CUDA (Compute Unified Device Architecture) in 2007, a software platform that allowed developers to use Nvidia's GPUs for general computing tasks, not just graphics.

The introduction of CUDA was a defining moment in Nvidia's history. It marked the company's transition into the world of AI and data centers. The high-performance computing capabilities of Nvidia's GPUs, combined with the CUDA platform, made it possible to process large and complex datasets more efficiently, accelerating the training and deployment of machine learning models. This development made Nvidia's technology essential for AI research and practical applications, ranging from autonomous vehicles to natural language processing.

In addition to GPUs, Nvidia also ventured into creating AI-specific hardware. This includes the Tesla accelerators designed for high-performance computing, the Jetson platform for AI at the edge, and the Titan series for AI research.

Furthermore, Nvidia also recognized the growing demand for powerful computing infrastructure in data centers. The company responded by offering a range of products and solutions tailored for data centers, including the Nvidia Data Center GPU Manager for monitoring and managing GPU servers and the A100 Tensor Core GPU, designed to handle diverse workloads in data centers.

In summary, Nvidia's technological journey has been a story of evolution and adaptation. The company's ability to pivot from being a graphics-focused company to becoming a key player in AI and data centers demonstrates its innovative spirit and foresight.

As AI continues to permeate various sectors, Nvidia's role in the tech industry is expected to continue growing.

Analysis of strategic shifts and innovations that propelled Nvidia to the forefront of the tech industry

Nvidia's rise to the forefront of the tech industry is a story of strategic shifts and groundbreaking innovations. From its early days as a graphics processing unit (GPU) manufacturer to its current standing as a leader in artificial intelligence (AI) technologies, Nvidia's journey is marked by bold decisions and pioneering advancements.

In the late 1990s, Nvidia made a strategic shift that would define its future. The company identified a growing demand for high-performance graphics processing to support the evolving needs of video games and professional visualization. In response, Nvidia introduced the GeForce 256, the world's first GPU. This innovative product offloaded graphics processing from the CPU, allowing for more complex and realistic graphics. This move not only established Nvidia as a leader in GPU technology but also set the stage for future advancements.

Another significant innovation came in 2006 with the launch of CUDA (Compute Unified Device Architecture), a software layer that gave developers direct access to the GPU's virtual instruction set and parallel computational elements. This innovation was a game-changer. It enabled the GPU to handle computational tasks traditionally reserved for the CPU, effectively turning the GPU into a general-purpose processor capable of handling a wide range of computing tasks.

In the mid-2010s, Nvidia made another strategic shift, this time towards AI and deep learning. The company recognized that GPUs, with their high-performance computing capabilities, were ideally suited to the parallel processing needs of deep learning algorithms. Nvidia began focusing on AI, creating hardware and software that made it easier for scientists and researchers to train neural networks. The company's GPU technology quickly became a key component in the infrastructure of leading AI research labs and tech companies.

Nvidia's foray into AI led to the development of new products like the Tesla and Titan GPUs, designed specifically for AI workloads, and the Drive platform for autonomous vehicles. Moreover, the company extended its reach into data centers, offering GPU-accelerated computing to drive efficiency and power in handling massive data workloads.

These strategic shifts and innovations were instrumental in propelling Nvidia to the forefront of the tech industry. By anticipating industry trends and investing in research and development, Nvidia has consistently pushed the boundaries of what's possible with GPU technology. The company's focus on AI and deep learning has positioned it at the center of a technological revolution, driving advancements in fields ranging from autonomous vehicles to healthcare to natural language processing.

Nvidia's trajectory is a testament to the power of innovation and strategic decision-making. Through its pioneering developments in GPU technology and its strategic focus on AI, Nvidia has shaped the tech industry and continues to drive the evolution of artificial intelligence.

CHAPTER 4:
POWERING THE GAME: NVIDIA'S IMPACT ON VIDEO GAMING

*Detailed exploration of
Nvidia's significant role in the
video gaming industry*

For over two decades, Nvidia has been at the forefront of the video gaming industry, revolutionizing the way games are developed, played, and experienced. From pioneering the first graphics processing unit (GPU) in 1999 to developing state-of-the-art technologies for real-time ray tracing, Nvidia's contributions to the video gaming industry are significant and far-reaching.

Nvidia's GPUs have been the backbone of high-performance gaming, allowing developers to create visually stunning and immersive games. The company's GeForce series, in particular, has been popular among gamers and developers alike. In 2023, Nvidia introduced the H100 GPU, designed to further enhance the gaming experience by boosting the computing speed of AI algorithms. This GPU forms the core of AI infrastructure, offering increased performance and efficiency.

Beyond hardware, Nvidia has made significant strides in software development, particularly in AI and machine learning. The company's AI technology has been harnessed to develop realistic and responsive in-game characters, improve graphics through deep learning super-sampling (DLSS), and enable real-time ray tracing for more immersive game environments.

In addition to this, Nvidia's open-source software has been a key driver for companies to use its chips. The company is looking to monetize its software business even more in the future, indicating a continued focus on software development for gaming and other applications.

Nvidia's influence also extends to cloud gaming services, where its GeForce NOW platform allows gamers to play their favorite PC games on nearly any device with high performance and visual fidelity. This service represents Nvidia's recognition of the growing trend of game streaming and its commitment to ensuring the best gaming experience for users regardless of their hardware.

Moving forward, Nvidia's continued innovation in both hardware and software positions the company to remain a dominant force in the video gaming industry. With a commitment to pushing the boundaries of what's possible in gaming, Nvidia continues to shape the future of this dynamic industry.

Examination of how Nvidia's GPUs revolutionized computer graphics and gaming experiences

Nvidia's journey in transforming computer graphics and gaming experiences began with the introduction of the world's first GPU, the GeForce 256, in 1999. The company coined the term 'GPU' to highlight the device's ability to offload geometric calculations from the CPU, thereby enabling more complex and realistic graphics.

The GeForce series of GPUs quickly became a staple in the gaming industry. Each new generation brought significant improvements in performance, allowing for more detailed graphics and smoother gameplay. The GPUs utilized advanced shading techniques to simulate realistic lighting and texture effects, giving rise to the era of 3D gaming.

However, the revolution didn't stop at graphics. Nvidia recognized early on the potential of harnessing GPU power for general-purpose computing tasks, leading to the development of CUDA (Compute Unified Device Architecture) in 2007. This platform allowed developers to leverage the parallel processing capabilities of Nvidia GPUs for a variety of applications beyond gaming, including AI and machine learning.

In 2018, Nvidia introduced real-time ray tracing with its Turing architecture, marking a significant leap forward in graphical realism. This technology simulates the physical behavior of light, rendering 3D environments with unparalleled detail and lifelike reflections, shadows, and refractions.

The impact of Nvidia's GPUs on gaming extends to AI as well. By incorporating AI technologies into its GPUs, Nvidia has helped create game characters that can learn, adapt, and respond in more human-like ways. This has significantly enhanced the interactive experience of games, making them more engaging and immersive.

In 2023, Nvidia announced the H100 GPU, setting a new benchmark for AI computing. The H100, along with the Grace CPU Superchip, forms the core of AI infrastructure, promising to reduce computing times and propel the development of complex AI algorithms. This evolution of Nvidia's GPUs is set to open new possibilities in gaming, potentially paving the way for more advanced AI interactions and even more realistic graphics.

Through these groundbreaking developments, Nvidia's GPUs have transformed the landscape of computer graphics and gaming experiences, continually pushing the boundaries of what is possible in virtual worlds.

Discussion of Nvidia's gaming-specific products, technologies, and partnerships

As a leading player in the gaming industry, Nvidia has introduced an array of gaming-specific products and technologies that have reshaped the landscape of video games.

GeForce GPUs: Nvidia's GeForce GPUs have been at the heart of PC gaming for decades. The GeForce series has consistently set new standards in graphics, performance, and power efficiency. With each new generation, gamers have been able to enjoy more detailed graphics, smoother gameplay, and more immersive experiences.

GeForce NOW: Recognizing the shift towards cloud gaming, Nvidia launched GeForce NOW, a cloud-based game streaming service. This platform allows gamers to play their favorite games on nearly any device, without the need for high-end gaming hardware. GeForce NOW leverages Nvidia's powerful data centers to run games at high settings and frame rates, streaming the gameplay to the user's device over the internet.

Nvidia G-Sync: To address the issue of screen tearing and stuttering in games, Nvidia introduced G-Sync. This technology synchronizes the display's refresh rate with the GPU's frame rate, resulting in smoother, tear-free gaming. G-Sync has been widely adopted by monitor manufacturers, enhancing the gaming experience for many players.

RTX Technology: With the introduction of the Turing architecture, Nvidia unveiled RTX technology, bringing real-time ray tracing to games. Ray tracing simulates the physical behavior of light to bring cinematic-quality graphics to gaming. RTX also includes DLSS (Deep Learning Super Sampling), an AI-powered technology that boosts frame rates while maintaining image quality.

Partnerships: Nvidia has formed strategic partnerships with various game developers and hardware manufacturers to optimize games for its GPUs and technologies. These partnerships have led to the release of 'RTX On' versions of popular games, featuring enhanced graphics with ray-traced effects and DLSS. Nvidia also collaborates with laptop and desktop manufacturers to provide gamers with a wide range of GeForce-powered systems.

In the automotive sector, Nvidia has partnered with car manufacturers like Mercedes-Benz, Volvo, and Tesla to bring advanced AI and visual computing capabilities to vehicles. In 2023, it was announced that Chinese electric vehicle maker BYD Co Ltd and luxury electric car maker Lucid Motors will be using Nvidia Drive for their next generation fleets, indicating the company's growing influence in the automotive industry.

Through its gaming-specific products, innovative technologies, and strategic partnerships, Nvidia continues to drive the evolution of the gaming industry, offering gamers ever-more sophisticated and immersive experiences.

Analysis of Nvidia's influence on emerging gaming trends, such as virtual reality and cloud gaming

The world of gaming is ever-evolving, with new trends and technologies emerging regularly. Nvidia, as a pioneering force in the gaming industry, has played a significant role in shaping these developments, particularly in the realms of virtual reality (VR) and cloud gaming.

Virtual Reality: VR offers gamers an immersive experience unlike any other, placing them inside the game world. However, VR demands high performance and low latency to ensure a smooth and responsive experience, challenging both hardware and software to keep up. Nvidia has risen to the task, with its GPUs providing the high-end performance required for VR. The company has also developed specific technologies for VR, such as VRWorks, which includes a suite of APIs, libraries, and engines that enable developers to create amazing VR experiences.

Nvidia's influence extends to the hardware used for VR as well. For example, Nvidia's partnership with Oculus, a leading VR headset manufacturer, has led to the optimization of VR experiences on Oculus devices when powered by Nvidia GPUs. By working closely with VR hardware manufacturers and game developers, Nvidia helps to ensure that VR gaming is a visually stunning and fluid experience.

Cloud Gaming: The rise of cloud gaming represents another major shift in the gaming landscape. By running games on powerful servers and streaming the gameplay to users' devices, cloud gaming allows high-end gaming experiences on a wide range of hardware, including low-end PCs, mobile devices, and smart TVs. Nvidia's GeForce NOW is a prime example of this trend. Leveraging Nvidia's powerful GPUs in data centers around the world, GeForce NOW delivers high-quality gaming experiences to users regardless of the capabilities of their local hardware.

Furthermore, Nvidia's GPUs, with their superior performance and efficiency, have become a popular choice for the data centers that power cloud gaming services. The company's advances in GPU technology have thus been integral to the growth and development of cloud gaming.

In both virtual reality and cloud gaming, Nvidia has shown its commitment to pushing the boundaries of what is possible in gaming. By continually advancing its technology and forming strategic partnerships, Nvidia helps to drive and shape these emerging trends, ensuring that gamers have access to the most immersive and flexible experiences possible.

*Insights into how Nvidia's work
in gaming continues to intersect
with its broader AI initiatives*

In the modern digital landscape, the lines between various sectors are increasingly blurring. Nvidia, a leader in both gaming and artificial intelligence, is at the forefront of this trend, with its work in these two areas often intersecting and reinforcing each other.

AI in Gaming: AI has become a key part of modern gaming, used to create more realistic graphics, smarter non-player characters, and more immersive virtual worlds. Nvidia's GPUs are not only the power behind high-end graphics but also play a crucial role in AI computations. For instance, Nvidia's Turing architecture, introduced in 2018, included dedicated tensor cores for AI processing, enabling features like real-time ray tracing and DLSS (Deep Learning Super Sampling). DLSS, in particular, uses AI to upscale lower-resolution images in real-time, providing gamers with higher-quality visuals without the performance hit usually associated with rendering at higher resolutions.

Nvidia's AI research also benefits game developers. The company offers various AI tools and libraries, such as Nvidia GameWorks, which developers can use to incorporate AI features into their games. In addition, Nvidia's AI research sometimes leads to new gaming technologies. For example, Nvidia's work on GANs (generative adversarial networks) led to the development of a tool that can automatically generate 3D models for game environments, potentially saving game artists significant time and effort.

Gaming in AI: Conversely, gaming also influences Nvidia's AI work. Video games are often used as training environments for AI models because they provide complex, dynamic worlds that can be easily controlled and manipulated. Nvidia's GPUs enable these

AI models to be trained more quickly and efficiently.

In addition, Nvidia's work on creating realistic game graphics can feed into its AI research. For example, the techniques used to generate realistic lighting and shadows in games can also be used in AI models that need to understand and replicate the physical properties of the real world.

Nvidia's simultaneous focus on gaming and AI creates a virtuous cycle, where advances in one area often lead to advances in the other. This convergence not only strengthens Nvidia's position in both gaming and AI but also fuels innovation, enabling the creation of more powerful and intelligent technologies that push the boundaries of what's possible in both sectors.

CHAPTER 5: PROOF OF WORK: NVIDIA AND CRYPTOCURRENCY MINING

Overview of the role of Nvidia's GPUs in cryptocurrency mining

This chapter explores the significant role Nvidia's GPUs play in the world of cryptocurrency mining. It delves into the intricacies of the process, the importance of GPUs in it, and how Nvidia's technological advancements have influenced this sector.

Understanding Cryptocurrency Mining: The chapter begins with an introduction to cryptocurrency mining, explaining the concept of Proof of Work (PoW), the consensus algorithm that underlies many cryptocurrencies, including Bitcoin and Ethereum. This section aims to give readers a clear understanding of what mining is, why it's necessary, and how it works.

The Role of GPUs in Mining: Here, we delve into the technical aspects of mining and the crucial role GPUs play in it. We explain how miners use GPUs to solve complex mathematical problems, validate transactions, and secure the cryptocurrency network. The focus is on why Nvidia's GPUs, with their high-performance computing capabilities, are particularly favored by miners.

Nvidia's Impact on the Mining Sector: This section focuses on Nvidia's significant influence on the cryptocurrency mining industry. It explores how the company's continual advancements in GPU technology have led to increases in mining efficiency and profitability. This part also discusses the challenges Nvidia faces, such as supply shortages and the environmental concerns associated with energy-intensive mining.

Case Study - Ethereum Mining: In this segment, we take a deep dive into Ethereum mining, one of the most popular uses of Nvidia GPUs. We examine how Nvidia's technology has been instrumental in supporting Ethereum's PoW model. The discussion also touches on Ethereum's planned transition to a Proof of Stake (PoS) model and what this could mean for Nvidia.

Nvidia's Response to Cryptocurrency Mining Demand: This part discusses Nvidia's response to the growing demand for its GPUs from cryptocurrency miners. We look at the company's efforts to balance the needs of its core gaming customers with those of the mining community, including the introduction of mining-specific GPUs and measures to limit the mining capabilities of certain gaming GPUs.

The Future of Nvidia in Cryptocurrency Mining: The chapter concludes with a look at the future, considering how Nvidia might continue to influence the cryptocurrency mining sector. It contemplates potential advancements in Nvidia's GPU technology and speculates about the future of mining as more cryptocurrencies consider moving away from PoW models.

By the end of the chapter, readers will have gained a comprehensive understanding of Nvidia's role in cryptocurrency mining, the challenges and opportunities it presents, and the potential future directions this relationship could take.

Examination of how Nvidia's GPUs facilitate the mining of Ethereum and other proof-of-work coins

This section of the chapter delves into the technical details of how Nvidia's GPUs are used in the mining of Ethereum and other Proof-of-Work coins.

The Mining Process: Here, we explain the mining process, emphasizing how miners use computational power to solve complex mathematical problems, known as "hash functions," that secure the network and validate transactions. We introduce the concept of "difficulty" in mining, which adjusts based on the total computational power of the network to ensure that new blocks are added approximately every ten minutes (in the case of Bitcoin) or fifteen seconds (for Ethereum).

The Role of GPUs: We then focus on why GPUs, and Nvidia's GPUs in particular, are well-suited for cryptocurrency mining. We explain that the process of mining essentially involves repeatedly performing hash functions until a solution is found. This task is parallel in nature, meaning that it can be broken into many smaller tasks that can be performed simultaneously. GPUs, originally designed for rendering graphics, are excellent at performing many simple calculations at the same time, making them ideal for the parallel task of mining.

Nvidia and Ethereum Mining: This section delves into the specifics of how Nvidia's GPUs are used to mine Ethereum. We discuss how the high memory bandwidth and computational power of Nvidia's GPUs make them efficient for Ethereum mining, which requires a lot of memory and computational resources. We also explain how the unique architecture of Nvidia's GPUs, such as the CUDA cores, contributes to their superior performance in mining tasks.

Nvidia and Other Proof-of-Work Coins: In this part, we discuss the use of Nvidia's GPUs in mining other Proof-of-Work coins, such as Bitcoin, Litecoin, and others. We note that while Bitcoin mining has largely moved to specialized hardware known as ASICs, many other PoW coins are still primarily mined with GPUs. We explore how the specific requirements of each coin's hash function can make certain GPUs more or less efficient for mining them.

The Impact of Mining on Nvidia: Finally, we discuss the impact of cryptocurrency mining on Nvidia as a company. We cover the increased demand for Nvidia's GPUs from miners and the resulting challenges in meeting this demand while also serving their core markets in gaming and professional graphics. We also discuss the measures Nvidia has taken in response, such as introducing mining-specific GPUs and limiting the mining performance of certain gaming GPUs.

Throughout this examination, readers will gain a detailed understanding of how Nvidia's GPUs facilitate the mining of Ethereum and other Proof-of-Work coins, and the implications of this role for Nvidia and the broader cryptocurrency landscape.

Discussion of the impact of cryptocurrency mining on Nvidia's business and strategies

Cryptocurrency mining, especially the mining of Ethereum and other proof-of-work coins, relies heavily on the computational power provided by Graphics Processing Units (GPUs). In this context, Nvidia's GPUs have emerged as one of the most popular choices for miners due to their high performance and efficiency.

Proof-of-work (PoW) is a consensus algorithm used by cryptocurrencies like Bitcoin and Ethereum. In PoW, miners compete to solve complex mathematical problems, and the first one to solve the problem gets the right to add a new block to the blockchain and receive the associated reward. These mathematical problems involve hashing data, and GPUs, with their ability to perform many calculations simultaneously, are well-suited for this task.

Ethereum, in particular, has been designed to be "memory-hard," which means it requires a significant amount of RAM in addition to raw processing power. This design decision was made to prevent the use of Application-Specific Integrated Circuits (ASICs), which are hardware devices designed to perform a specific task (like Bitcoin mining) very efficiently, but which are out of reach for most casual users due to their high cost. By making Ethereum memory-hard, the developers ensured that GPUs, which have both processing power and RAM, would be the most efficient hardware for mining Ethereum.

Nvidia's GPUs, with their high performance and memory capacity, are ideal for this task. For example, the Nvidia GeForce GTX 1070, a popular choice among Ethereum miners, comes with 8 GB of GDDR5 memory and a base clock speed of 1506 MHz, making it capable of performing the calculations required for Ethereum mining efficiently.

However, the use of GPUs for cryptocurrency mining has also led to some challenges. The high demand from miners has often led to shortages, leaving gamers, who are the traditional users of GPUs, struggling to find available units. This has also led to inflated prices, as the demand for GPUs outstripped supply.

In response, Nvidia has taken steps to address these issues, including manufacturing GPUs specifically designed for cryptocurrency mining. These GPUs, called Cryptocurrency Mining Processors (CMPs), are optimized for mining performance and efficiency but do not include display outputs, making them unsuitable for gaming. This allows Nvidia to better meet the demands of both miners and gamers, though it remains a delicate balancing act.

The fact that Nvidia's GPUs are being used to power the crypto-mining industry is another testament to their versatility and performance. It also underscores the pivotal role that Nvidia plays in various sectors, from gaming and AI to cryptocurrency.

In-depth analysis of the technological aspects of cryptocurrency mining, with a particular focus on how Nvidia's GPUs are used in this process

Cryptocurrency mining, particularly in proof-of-work systems, involves solving complex mathematical problems, known as hashes. These problems require an immense amount of computational power to solve, as they involve searching for a specific number in a vast numerical landscape.

Proof-of-work systems are designed so that solving these problems is difficult, but verifying a solution is relatively easy. This asymmetry is what allows the blockchain to maintain its integrity: while it takes a significant amount of processing power to add a new block to the chain, any participant in the network can easily check the validity of a new block once it has been added.

Nvidia's GPUs are well-suited to this type of work because they are designed for parallel processing. In contrast to a CPU (Central Processing Unit), which is designed to handle a few complex tasks at a time, a GPU is built to manage many simple tasks simultaneously. This is because GPUs were originally designed to handle the rendering of images and video, which involves performing similar calculations on large sets of pixels concurrently.

In the context of cryptocurrency mining, this means that a GPU can compute many hashes simultaneously. Since finding the correct hash is largely a matter of trial and error, being able to check many possibilities at once greatly increases the efficiency of the process.

Nvidia's GPUs, in particular, are favored for their high performance and energy efficiency. These qualities make them cost-effective for mining operations, which typically involve running many GPUs continuously for long periods of time. The high memory bandwidth of Nvidia's GPUs also makes them well-suited to mining algorithms that are memory-intensive, such as Ethereum's Ethash.

Furthermore, Nvidia's software ecosystem provides additional advantages for miners. The CUDA platform, for instance, allows developers to write software that takes full advantage of Nvidia's GPUs, further enhancing their performance in mining applications.

In summary, Nvidia's GPUs, with their parallel processing capabilities, high performance, and robust software support, are a cornerstone technology in the world of cryptocurrency mining.

Insights into the challenges and opportunities that the crypto-mining boom presents for Nvidia

The boom in cryptocurrency mining has presented both opportunities and challenges for Nvidia.

Opportunities:

Increased Demand: The high demand for GPUs in cryptocurrency mining has led to increased sales and revenue for Nvidia. The company's powerful and energy-efficient GPUs have become highly sought after by miners.

New Market: Cryptocurrency mining has opened up a new market for Nvidia. Initially, Nvidia GPUs were primarily used by gamers and professionals in fields such as design and animation. The rise of cryptocurrency mining has created an entirely new category of customers for the company.

Technological Innovation: The demand for more efficient mining hardware has pushed Nvidia to innovate and create new, more powerful GPUs. The company has also developed mining-specific

GPUs, which are optimized for the demands of cryptocurrency mining.

Challenges:

Supply and Demand Imbalance: The surge in demand for Nvidia GPUs for mining has often outstripped supply, leading to shortages. This has caused frustration among Nvidia's core customer base of gamers, who have found it difficult to purchase GPUs at reasonable prices.

Market Volatility: The cryptocurrency market is known for its volatility. This presents a risk for Nvidia, as a downturn in the market could lead to a sudden drop in demand for GPUs for mining.

Regulatory Uncertainty: Cryptocurrencies are subject to regulatory scrutiny and potential regulatory action in many jurisdictions. This regulatory uncertainty could affect the demand for GPUs for mining.

E-Waste and Environmental Concerns: The rapid cycle of hardware upgrades in the mining sector contributes to electronic waste. Additionally, the energy use involved in mining is substantial, leading to concerns about the environmental impact of mining activities. These issues could lead to reputational risks for Nvidia and potentially increased regulatory scrutiny.

In response to these challenges and opportunities, Nvidia has been balancing its product offerings, creating GPUs specifically for miners while also trying to ensure that gamers and other customers can still get the products they need. The company continues to innovate and adapt to the evolving needs of both the gaming and mining sectors.

Discussion of Nvidia's responses to these developments

Nvidia has taken several measures in response to the unprecedented demand for its GPUs from cryptocurrency miners and the subsequent challenges this has posed for the gaming community.

Release of Mining-Specific GPUs: In an attempt to prevent miners from purchasing GPUs intended for gamers, Nvidia has released Cryptocurrency Mining Processors (CMPs). These GPUs are specifically designed for the needs of cryptocurrency mining. They lack display outputs and other features that are essential for gamers but unnecessary for miners, making them less attractive to the gaming community. By creating a separate line of products tailored to miners, Nvidia aims to ensure that gaming GPUs go to gamers, and mining GPUs go to miners.

Software Limitations: Nvidia has implemented measures to make its gaming GPUs less attractive to miners. For example, the company has released driver updates that limit the hash rate, or mining efficiency, of certain GPUs when they are used to mine Ethereum, a popular cryptocurrency. This makes these GPUs less efficient for mining and thus less desirable to miners, while not affecting their performance for gaming.

Transparency and Communication: Nvidia has been open about the challenges it is facing in meeting the demand for its GPUs and its efforts to address these challenges. The company has communicated its strategies and plans to its customers and stakeholders, helping to manage expectations and alleviate frustration.

R&D Investment: Nvidia continues to invest in research and development to drive innovation and create more efficient, powerful GPUs for both gaming and mining. This not only helps to meet the growing demand for GPUs but also allows Nvidia to stay competitive in a rapidly evolving market.

Strategic Partnerships: Nvidia has also been working with retailers and distributors to prevent bulk buying and to ensure that its GPUs are more accessible to gamers. For example, some retailers are offering priority access or bundling GPUs with other gaming components to deter miners.

These measures highlight Nvidia's proactive and balanced approach in addressing the needs of both its gaming and mining customers.

Examination of the broader implications of Nvidia's involvement in cryptocurrency mining for the tech industry and the future of digital currencies

Nvidia's involvement in cryptocurrency mining has broad implications for both the tech industry and the future of digital currencies.

Tech Industry: The demand for Nvidia's GPUs for cryptocurrency mining has highlighted the intersection of the tech and cryptocurrency sectors. This has brought new attention and resources to both industries, fostering innovation and growth. Nvidia's involvement in cryptocurrency mining has also highlighted the need for more efficient and sustainable technologies, given the high energy consumption of cryptocurrency mining. This could spur further research and development in energy-efficient computing technologies. Additionally, Nvidia's response to the demands of cryptocurrency mining, such as the development of mining-specific GPUs, illustrates the potential for tech companies to create specialized products for niche markets.

Future of Digital Currencies: Nvidia's GPUs play a crucial role in maintaining the security and integrity of proof-of-work cryptocurrencies like Bitcoin and Ethereum. By providing the computing power needed for mining, these GPUs help to validate transactions and add them to the blockchain, a key process in the operation of these digital currencies. As such, the future of these cryptocurrencies may be closely tied to the availability and performance of mining hardware like Nvidia's GPUs. Nvidia's involvement in cryptocurrency mining could also influence the direction of these digital currencies. For example, if Nvidia were to develop more efficient mining hardware, it could potentially influence the debate between proof-of-work and more energy-efficient consensus mechanisms like proof-of-stake.

Sustainability: Nvidia's role in cryptocurrency mining also raises important questions about sustainability. Cryptocurrency mining is known for its high energy consumption, leading to concerns about its environmental impact. If Nvidia can develop more energy-efficient GPUs or alternatives for mining, it could help mitigate these environmental concerns, influencing the sustainability of the tech industry and digital currencies.

Overall, Nvidia's involvement in cryptocurrency mining is shaping the future of both the tech industry and digital currencies in significant ways. As the company continues to innovate and respond to market demands, it will likely continue to influence these sectors.

CHAPTER 6: THE SCIENCE OF AI: COMPUTING AND PROCESSING WITH CHIPS

Explanation of the computational and processing aspects of AI

Artificial Intelligence (AI) involves creating systems that can perform tasks that normally require human intelligence, such as understanding natural language, recognizing patterns, solving problems, and making decisions. These tasks often involve complex mathematical computations and the processing of large amounts of data, requiring considerable computational power.

There are several key computational and processing aspects in AI:

Data Processing: AI systems learn and make decisions based on data. They require the ability to process and analyze large volumes of data quickly and accurately. This is particularly true for machine learning, a subset of AI, where algorithms learn from data and improve their performance over time.

Parallel Processing: AI computations often involve performing the same operation on multiple data points simultaneously, a process known as parallel processing. This is especially important in tasks such as image and speech recognition, where thousands or even millions of data points (pixels in an image or audio signals in speech) need to be processed at once.

High Performance Computing (HPC): AI computations can be incredibly complex and may require high performance computing capabilities. HPC involves the use of supercomputers and parallel processing techniques to solve complex computational problems quickly.

Graphics Processing Units (GPUs): GPUs, originally designed for rendering graphics in video games, have become an essential tool in AI computations. GPUs are capable of performing many calculations simultaneously, making them well-suited for the parallel processing needs of AI.

Neural Networks and Deep Learning: Many AI systems use artificial neural networks, particularly deep learning models, to perform tasks. These models involve many layers of interconnected nodes (or "neurons") and require substantial computational resources to train and operate.

Hardware Accelerators: As AI computations have become more complex, there has been a growing demand for specialized hardware accelerators. These devices, such as Tensor Processing Units (TPUs) or Application-Specific Integrated Circuits (ASICs), are designed to accelerate specific types of AI computations.

In summary, the computational and processing aspects of AI involve handling large volumes of data, performing complex mathematical computations, and using parallel processing techniques. These requirements have driven the development of specialized hardware and software tools designed to facilitate and accelerate AI computations.

Discussion of the role of chips in AI, and the specifics of how they facilitate AI technologies

Artificial Intelligence (AI) has revolutionized the technology industry, and at the heart of this revolution are chips, more specifically, Graphics Processing Units (GPUs) and Tensor Processing Units (TPUs). These chips play a crucial role in AI technologies, enabling the computational power required to process vast amounts of data and execute complex algorithms.

AI involves mimicking human intelligence processes by machines, particularly computer systems. These processes include learning (acquiring information and the rules for using the information), reasoning (using the rules to reach approximate or definite conclusions), and self-correction. These operations demand enormous computational power, which is facilitated by specialized chips.

GPUs, originally designed for rendering graphics in computer games, have been repurposed for AI due to their ability to perform many calculations simultaneously. Traditional Central Processing Units (CPUs) are excellent for executing single-threaded tasks or tasks with a small number of threads, but they struggle with the massive parallelism required in AI workloads. GPUs, on the other hand, are designed to handle thousands of threads at once, making them ideal for the parallel computations that power deep learning and other AI algorithms.

Nvidia, a leading player in the GPU market, has been instrumental in this shift. The company's GPUs, combined with its CUDA programming model, have become a standard in AI research and development. Nvidia's CUDA platform allows developers to use GPUs for general-purpose computing, including the computation-heavy task of training deep learning models.

Tensor Processing Units (TPUs), on the other hand, are specialized chips designed specifically for accelerating machine learning workloads. They are built to handle the high computational demands of AI operations, particularly tensor operations that are common in deep learning algorithms. TPUs are highly efficient at matrix operations, which are at the heart of neural network computations.

In addition to GPUs and TPUs, specialized AI chips such as Nvidia's Tensor Cores are designed to accelerate specific types of AI workloads. Tensor Cores, for instance, are designed to speed up the training and inference of large AI models by performing mixed-precision matrix multiply and accumulate calculations in a single operation.

In summary, chips play a fundamental role in AI technologies. By providing the computational power needed to process large datasets and execute complex algorithms, chips like GPUs, TPUs, and specialized AI chips enable the development and deployment of AI technologies. As AI continues to evolve and push the boundaries of what's possible, the role of these chips will only become more critical.

An overview of the evolution
of AI chips, focusing on
Nvidia's contributions

The evolution of Artificial Intelligence (AI) chips is a story of relentless innovation and adaptation to meet the ever-growing computational demands of AI applications. Nvidia, with its pioneering technology and visionary leadership, has played a significant role in this evolution.

The early years of AI research did not involve specialized chips. Instead, general-purpose central processing units (CPUs) were used. However, CPUs, designed to handle a broad range of tasks efficiently, were not optimized for the specific demands of AI computations, which often involve processing large amounts of data in parallel.

The first major shift came with the realization that graphics processing units (GPUs), originally designed for rendering video game graphics, were well-suited for AI computations. GPUs, with their hundreds or even thousands of cores capable of performing calculations simultaneously, were perfect for the parallel processing requirements of AI algorithms.

Nvidia, a leading manufacturer of GPUs, was at the forefront of this shift. Recognizing the potential of their GPUs for AI, Nvidia introduced CUDA (Compute Unified Device Architecture) in 2007. CUDA is a software platform that allows developers to use Nvidia's GPUs for general computing tasks, effectively turning them into multi-purpose processors capable of handling the computations required by AI algorithms.

The advent of CUDA represented a major milestone in the evolution of AI chips. Nvidia's GPUs, combined with the CUDA platform, became a fundamental tool for AI researchers and developers, enabling faster and more efficient processing of AI workloads.

Following the success of GPUs in AI, the demand for even more specialized hardware grew. This led to the development of AI-specific chips, such as Tensor Processing Units (TPUs) and Application-Specific Integrated Circuits (ASICs). These chips are designed specifically to accelerate certain types of AI computations, such as those used in deep learning algorithms.

In response to this trend, Nvidia expanded its product line to include AI-specific hardware. Notable examples include the Tesla accelerators designed for high-performance computing and the Titan series for AI research. More recently, Nvidia introduced the A100 Tensor Core GPU, which is designed to handle a diverse range of workloads in data centers, including AI computations.

In summary, the evolution of AI chips has been characterized by a shift from general-purpose CPUs to GPUs and then to more specialized AI chips. Throughout this evolution, Nvidia has been a key contributor, driving innovation and providing technologies that have significantly advanced the capabilities of AI systems.

Update with information about Nvidia's 2023 introduction of new chips

In 2023, Nvidia made significant strides in AI hardware technology. The company announced the introduction of new chips, including the H100 GPU and the Grace CPU Superchip. These advanced chips were developed with the specific aim of boosting the computing speed of increasingly complex AI algorithms.

The H100 GPU serves as the core of AI infrastructure, emphasizing Nvidia's commitment to advancing AI technology. Concurrently, the Grace CPU Superchip marks Nvidia's first Arm-based chip released after its attempt to acquire Arm Ltd fell apart.

These developments underscore Nvidia's continuous innovation in AI processing. The advanced capabilities of these new chips aim to reduce computing times from weeks to days for some work involving the training of AI models, making them a significant addition to the AI ecosystem.

CHAPTER 7: THE HEART OF AI: NVIDIA'S CHIPS

Detailed exploration of Nvidia's AI chips, their functionality, and their importance in AI technologies

Nvidia has been a pioneering force in the development of chips tailored for Artificial Intelligence (AI) applications. The company's chips, including the flagship Tesla and Titan GPUs, as well as more recent innovations like the A100 Tensor Core GPU and the Jetson platform for edge computing, have set the standard in AI computing.

Nvidia's Tesla GPUs, named after the physicist Nikola Tesla, were among the first to be specifically designed for accelerating AI workloads. They are packed with thousands of CUDA cores, a specialized architecture designed for parallel processing. Tesla GPUs are widely used in AI research and in the data centers of tech giants for their ability to accelerate deep learning and other AI tasks.

Nvidia's Titan GPUs, while also popular in gaming, have become a go-to choice for AI researchers and professionals who require powerful processing capabilities on their personal workstations. Titan GPUs are particularly effective for training deep learning models and running complex simulations.

In 2020, Nvidia introduced the A100 Tensor Core GPU, the company's first GPU based on the Ampere architecture. The A100 represents a significant leap in power and efficiency. It is equipped with Tensor Cores, which are designed to accelerate tensor operations in deep learning algorithms, and Multi-Instance GPU (MIG) technology, which allows a single A100 GPU to be partitioned into as many as seven separate GPUs to better allocate resources for diverse workloads.

Beyond the data center, Nvidia has also developed chips for edge computing. The Jetson platform is a series of small, power-efficient modules designed for AI applications in robotics, drones, and other autonomous machines. Jetson modules are capable of running AI algorithms in real-time, making them ideal for use cases where data needs to be processed on the device rather than being sent to a remote data center.

The functionality of Nvidia's AI chips extends to software as well. Nvidia's CUDA platform allows developers to use the company's GPUs for general-purpose computing, while libraries like cuDNN and TensorRT provide tools for designing and optimizing deep learning models.

Nvidia's AI chips are more than just hardware; they represent an ecosystem of technologies designed to facilitate AI research and development. These chips are not only important for running AI technologies; they are actively shaping the evolution of AI. Through its innovative chips, Nvidia is enabling more complex and powerful AI models, driving advancements in fields ranging from autonomous vehicles to healthcare, and helping to realize the potential of AI.

Analysis of Nvidia's impact in the AI landscape through its chip technology

Nvidia's contributions to the field of Artificial Intelligence (AI) have been transformative, shaping the way AI systems are built and operate. The company's chip technology, in particular, has played a crucial role in enabling the growth and advancement of AI.

Enabling Parallel Processing with GPUs: Nvidia's Graphics Processing Units (GPUs) were a game-changer for AI computations. With their ability to perform many calculations simultaneously, GPUs are ideally suited to the parallel processing requirements of AI algorithms. This capability has significantly accelerated the training and operation of AI models, enabling more complex and capable AI systems to be developed.

Introduction of CUDA: Nvidia's Compute Unified Device Architecture (CUDA) marked a turning point in the use of GPUs for AI. CUDA is a software platform that allows developers to use Nvidia's GPUs for general computing tasks, effectively turning GPUs into multi-purpose processors capable of handling the computations required by AI algorithms. CUDA has made it easier for AI researchers and developers to leverage the power of GPUs, democratizing access to high-performance computing and accelerating the pace of AI innovation.

Development of AI-Specific Hardware: Recognizing the need for more specialized hardware for AI computations, Nvidia has developed a range of products specifically designed for AI workloads. These include the Tesla accelerators for high-performance computing, the Titan series for AI research, and more recently, the A100 Tensor Core GPU for data centers. These products have provided AI researchers and developers with powerful tools to train and operate increasingly complex AI models.

Supporting AI Infrastructure: Nvidia's chip technology has not only supported the development of AI models but also the infrastructure required to run these models. The company's data center solutions, powered by its GPUs, have been crucial in handling the high computational demands of AI applications, enabling more robust and scalable AI systems.

Fostering AI Research and Development: Through its hardware and software offerings, Nvidia has fostered AI research and development. The company's technology has been used in a wide range of AI applications, from autonomous vehicles and robotics to healthcare and natural language processing.

In conclusion, Nvidia's impact on the AI landscape through its chip technology has been profound. The company's innovations have accelerated the development and deployment of AI, enabling breakthroughs in a wide range of fields. As the demand for AI continues to grow, Nvidia's role in shaping the AI landscape is set to continue.

Details about the specific chips announced in 2023, their functionality, and their role in advancing AI infrastructure

In 2023, Nvidia continued to push the boundaries of AI infrastructure with the introduction of the H100 GPU and the Grace CPU Superchip. These new chips were designed to significantly enhance AI processing capabilities, signifying another milestone in Nvidia's ongoing commitment to AI technology.

The H100 GPU, described by Nvidia's CEO Jensen Huang as the "engine" of AI infrastructure, is an advanced graphics processing unit built to handle the complex computations required in AI applications. Its design allows for the acceleration of AI training and inference, making it a critical component in AI data centers and cloud computing.

On the other hand, the Grace CPU Superchip is Nvidia's first Arm-based chip, marking a significant expansion of Nvidia's product portfolio. This superchip is designed to work in harmony with Nvidia's GPUs, aiming to provide a holistic and optimized processing solution for AI tasks. The Grace CPU Superchip's integration of Arm technology indicates Nvidia's strategic direction following the collapse of its deal to acquire Arm Ltd.

Together, the H100 GPU and the Grace CPU Superchip offer a robust hardware foundation for AI applications. By reducing computing times from weeks to days for certain AI training tasks, these chips stand to revolutionize the efficiency and speed of AI operations, bolstering Nvidia's position as a key innovator in the AI chip market.

CHAPTER 8: THE AI BOOM: NVIDIA'S INTEGRAL ROLE

Comprehensive account of the rapid growth of AI in recent years and Nvidia's role in this expansion

Artificial Intelligence (AI) has experienced a meteoric rise in recent years. From voice assistants and recommendation algorithms to autonomous vehicles and healthcare diagnostics, AI technologies have permeated virtually every industry. Central to this expansion has been Nvidia, a company whose hardware and software innovations have been instrumental in powering the AI boom.

The rapid growth of AI has been driven by a convergence of factors. The explosion of data, advancements in machine learning algorithms, and improvements in computing power have all contributed to the proliferation of AI technologies. However, the realization of these technologies would not have been possible without the necessary hardware to process vast amounts of data and perform complex computations - and that's where Nvidia comes in.

Nvidia's graphics processing units (GPUs), originally designed for rendering graphics in video games, have found a new purpose in AI. GPUs are particularly well-suited for AI workloads due to their ability to perform many calculations simultaneously, which is essential for training deep learning models. Nvidia's GPUs, combined with its CUDA programming model, have become a standard in AI research and development, enabling scientists and engineers to train larger and more complex models than ever before.

But Nvidia's contribution to the AI boom goes beyond GPUs. The company has developed a suite of hardware and software products tailored for AI applications. The Tesla and Titan GPUs, the A100 Tensor Core GPU, and the Jetson platform for edge computing are all part of Nvidia's AI ecosystem. On the software side, Nvidia provides tools like cuDNN and TensorRT that help developers design and optimize deep learning models.

Nvidia's role in the AI boom extends to its collaborations with leading AI research labs and tech companies. Nvidia's hardware powers some of the world's most powerful supercomputers, which are used for cutting-edge AI research. The company also partners with tech giants like Google and Facebook, providing the hardware infrastructure that powers their AI services.

In summary, Nvidia has played an integral role in the rapid growth of AI in recent years. The company's hardware and software innovations have enabled the development and deployment of AI technologies, driving advancements across various industries. As AI continues to evolve, Nvidia's contributions will undoubtedly remain at the forefront of this technological revolution.

Examination of the influence of this growth on Nvidia's reputation, financial performance, and influence in the tech industry

Financial Performance: Nvidia's financial performance has seen some fluctuations. In the fourth quarter of fiscal 2023, the company reported quarterly revenue of $6.05 billion, down 21% from a year ago, and fiscal-year revenue of $27.0 billion, which remained flat from the previous year. The company's GAAP earnings per diluted share for the fourth quarter were $0.57, down 52% from a year ago. However, Nvidia's revenue for the first quarter of fiscal 2024 was expected to be $6.50 billion, showing some growth from the previous quarter. In the first quarter of fiscal 2024, Nvidia's earnings beat estimates, with adjusted earnings per share of $0.90, up from $0.73 per share in the year-ago quarter.

Reputation and Influence in the Tech Industry: Despite some financial fluctuations, Nvidia's influence in the tech industry remains significant. The company continues to pioneer and expand its offerings in AI and large language models. Nvidia's CEO, Jensen Huang, noted an "accelerated interest in the versatility and capabilities of generative AI" from startups to major enterprises. Nvidia is partnering with leading cloud service providers to offer AI-as-a-service, providing enterprises with access to its AI platform, which includes its new AI supercomputer, the AI supercomputer through the NVIDIA DGX Cloud, and customizable AI models. This suggests a strong reputation and influence in the field of AI and related technologies .

CHAPTER 9: THE GENERATIVE AI REVOLUTION AND NVIDIA'S PIONEERING ROLE

Explanation of generative AI and
its potential for transformation
in various industries

Generative AI represents a cutting-edge development in artificial intelligence that has the potential to revolutionize various industries. Unlike traditional AI models that make decisions or predictions based on input data, generative models are capable of creating new, original content. They can generate everything from images, music, and text to 3D models and synthetic data.

Generative AI works by learning the underlying patterns in the data it is trained on and then using that knowledge to generate new, similar data. This is achieved through a type of machine learning model called a Generative Adversarial Network (GAN). A GAN consists of two parts: a generator, which creates new data, and a discriminator, which tries to distinguish the generated data from the real data. Through a process of competition and cooperation, the generator gradually improves its ability to produce realistic data.

The potential of generative AI for transformation in various industries is vast. In the creative industries, for instance, generative AI can be used to create original music, artwork, and design elements. In healthcare, generative models can synthesize medical data or generate 3D models of organs for surgical planning. In the automotive industry, generative AI can be used to simulate different driving scenarios for training autonomous vehicles.

Nvidia has been a key player in the development and application of generative AI. The company's GPUs, with their high-performance computing capabilities, are ideally suited to the demanding computational needs of GANs. Nvidia has also developed software tools that help researchers and developers build and optimize generative models.

Moreover, Nvidia has showcased the potential of generative AI through its own research. The company has developed advanced GANs that can generate highly realistic images and even simulate virtual worlds. These developments not only demonstrate the capabilities of generative AI but also point to the transformative potential of this technology in various industries. As generative AI continues to evolve, Nvidia's hardware and software innovations will likely continue to play a pivotal role in driving this revolution.

Exploration of Nvidia's involvement with generative AI, its collaborations with leading AI organizations, and its role in revolutionary technologies like ChatGPT

Nvidia has been at the forefront of pioneering research in AI, particularly in generative AI, which has become a transformative force in various industries. The company has introduced a wave of cutting-edge AI research, advancing generative AI and neural graphics in collaboration with numerous universities worldwide. Some of their key research papers have focused on generative AI models that turn text into personalized images, inverse rendering tools transforming still images into 3D objects, neural physics models simulating complex 3D elements with stunning realism, and neural rendering models that generate real-time, AI-powered visual details. These research advancements have significant implications for various fields, including art, architecture, graphic design, game development, film, and even robotics and autonomous vehicle training.

Nvidia's generative AI models are powerful tools that transform text into images, providing inspiration and creative options for concept art or storyboards for films, video games, and 3D virtual worlds. For instance, a creative director for a toy brand could visualize a new teddy bear in various situations. A collaborative research project between Tel Aviv University and Nvidia has led to the development of techniques that enable a high level of specificity in the output of a generative AI model. These techniques allow users to provide image examples that the model quickly learns from, leading to highly personalized output.

Beyond image generation, Nvidia's research in AI is also paving the way for transforming 2D images and videos into 3D representations. One groundbreaking technique can generate and render a photorealistic 3D head-and-shoulders model based on a single 2D portrait, making 3D avatar creation and 3D video conferencing more accessible with AI.

In a collaboration with Stanford University, Nvidia's research has enabled lifelike motion for 3D characters by creating an AI system that can learn a range of skills from 2D video recordings and apply them to 3D characters. This research addresses the challenge of producing 3D characters that can perform diverse skills with realistic movement without the use of expensive motion-capture data.

Nvidia has also showcased a method that can simulate tens of thousands of hairs in high resolution and in real time using neural physics, an AI technique that teaches a neural network to predict how an object would move in the real world. This method is specifically optimized for modern GPUs, offering significant performance leaps and quality boosts compared to previous solutions.

After an environment is filled with animated 3D objects and characters, Nvidia's research in real-time rendering simulates the physics of light reflecting through the virtual scene. The company's latest neural rendering inventions extend programmable shading code with AI models that run deep inside Nvidia's real-time graphics pipelines, delivering film-quality, photorealistic visuals in real time for video games and digital twins.

Through their innovative research and collaborations, Nvidia continues to play a pivotal role in the advancement of AI technologies, including generative AI and tools like ChatGPT.

CHAPTER 10: NVIDIA'S COMPETITIVE EDGE IN THE AI CHIP INDUSTRY

Analytical look at Nvidia's position
and strengths in the AI chip market

As of 2023, Nvidia's position in the AI chip market is both dominant and promising. With a market capitalization of nearly $939 billion, Nvidia stands as the fifth most valuable U.S. company and twice as big as the second-largest chip firm, Taiwan's TSMC. In the United States, it only trails the trillion-dollar-value companies such as Apple, Alphabet, Microsoft, and Amazon. This dominance is particularly pronounced in the market for chips used to power AI services, where Nvidia is seen as a leader.

Nvidia's strength lies not only in its current market position but also in its future potential, underpinned by the ongoing AI boom. CEO Jensen Huang has suggested that $1 trillion worth of current equipment in data centers would have to be replaced with AI chips, in line with the increasing application of generative AI in various products and services. This paints a picture of immense market opportunity for Nvidia and a potential for growth that some analysts compare to significant inflection points in technological history, such as the advent of the internal combustion engine or the internet.

What sets Nvidia apart is not just its size, but its strategic positioning at the intersection of multiple growth trajectories in the tech industry. By being at the forefront of the AI revolution and leading the way in AI chip development, Nvidia has carved out a unique and enviable position that places it at the heart of the AI landscape. This strategic advantage, combined with a demonstrated capacity for innovation and adaptation, positions Nvidia to continue playing a significant role in shaping the future of AI.

*Exploration of the unique
capabilities and attributes
that give Nvidia a competitive
advantage in AI processing*

Nvidia's competitive advantage in AI processing stems from a combination of unique capabilities and attributes:

Industry-Leading GPUs: Nvidia has been a pioneer in developing Graphics Processing Units (GPUs) that are instrumental in AI processing. GPUs are ideal for AI tasks due to their parallel processing capabilities, which allows them to handle multiple computations simultaneously. This makes them particularly suited to the matrix and vector operations common in machine learning and deep learning applications. Nvidia's cutting-edge GPUs, like the Tesla V100 and the A100, have set the industry standard for AI computing power.

CUDA Software: Nvidia's Compute Unified Device Architecture (CUDA) is a proprietary parallel computing platform and API that allows developers to use Nvidia GPUs for general purpose processing. CUDA's deep integration with Nvidia hardware and broad adoption by AI software platforms such as TensorFlow and PyTorch have made Nvidia GPUs a go-to choice for many AI applications.

AI-Specific Hardware Innovations: Nvidia has also developed hardware specifically tailored to AI workloads. For example, the Tensor Cores in their Volta and newer architectures are designed to accelerate the matrix operations that are common in deep learning, offering a significant performance boost over traditional GPU cores for these tasks.

Comprehensive AI Platform: Beyond hardware, Nvidia offers a comprehensive AI platform that includes software tools, libraries, and frameworks designed to help developers and researchers build and deploy AI models. This ecosystem, combined with their powerful hardware, provides a complete solution for AI workloads.

Strategic Partnerships and Acquisitions: Nvidia has established strategic partnerships with key players in various sectors, and has made acquisitions that strengthen its position in the AI landscape. The proposed acquisition of Arm Ltd., for example, could potentially expand Nvidia's reach into a vast range of devices and applications.

AI Research and Development: Nvidia is heavily invested in AI research and development, contributing to both applied and fundamental AI research. This not only helps in advancing the state of AI technology but also ensures Nvidia stays at the forefront of the field.

Cloud AI Services: Nvidia has partnered with leading cloud service providers to offer AI-as-a-service. This provides enterprises access to Nvidia's world-leading AI platform, offering options to engage each layer of Nvidia AI - the AI supercomputer, acceleration libraries software, or pretrained generative AI models - as a cloud service. This allows a broad range of customers to take advantage of Nvidia's AI technology, even if they don't have the resources to invest in hardware themselves.

These unique capabilities and attributes have positioned Nvidia as a leader in the AI processing landscape. Its continued innovation and strategic positioning suggest it will continue to play a crucial role in the advancement and deployment of AI technologies.

CHAPTER 11: THE ADVENT OF ROBOTICS: NVIDIA'S EARLY CONTRIBUTIONS

Detailed account of Nvidia's initial foray into the field of robotics

In the early 2010s, Nvidia recognized the transformative potential of robotics and began to shift its focus in this direction. The company, already a global leader in graphics processing units (GPUs) for gaming and professional markets, saw robotics as a natural progression of its business. Robotics provided a new frontier for Nvidia's processing power, which was already known for its ability to perform complex computations quickly and efficiently.

Nvidia's initial foray into the field of robotics was marked by a series of strategic decisions and partnerships. The company started by incorporating robotics applications into its existing GPU technology. This approach leveraged the high processing capabilities of GPUs, making them ideal for the complex computations required in robotics. The company's GPUs were used to power autonomous robots, enabling them to perceive their environment, navigate through it, and perform tasks.

In 2015, Nvidia introduced the Jetson TX1, a mini supercomputer designed specifically for machine learning and AI applications. This compact module provided the processing power needed for autonomous machines and intelligent devices, marking a major milestone in Nvidia's foray into the field of robotics.

In addition to developing its own technologies, Nvidia also established partnerships with several leading robotics companies and research institutions. These collaborations allowed Nvidia to gain access to advanced robotics technologies and to influence the development of new systems and applications.

One such partnership was with Fanuc, a leading supplier of robotics, CNC systems, and factory automation. In 2016, Nvidia and Fanuc announced a collaboration to implement AI capabilities in Fanuc's manufacturing robots using Nvidia's AI platform. This marked a significant step in Nvidia's push into the robotics industry, demonstrating the practical applications of its technology in an industrial setting.

Overall, Nvidia's initial foray into robotics was characterized by a combination of technological innovation, strategic partnerships, and a clear vision for the future of the industry. This approach allowed the company to establish a strong foothold in the robotics field, setting the stage for the significant contributions it would make in the years to come.

Analysis of the technologies and strategies that have driven Nvidia's success in this arena

Nvidia's success in the robotics arena can be attributed to a combination of innovative technologies, strategic partnerships, and an understanding of the rapidly evolving landscape of AI and robotics. The company's approach to robotics was rooted in its existing strengths in GPU technology and AI, which allowed it to develop unique solutions for the challenges posed by robotics.

GPU Technology

At the heart of Nvidia's success in robotics is its GPU technology. GPUs, originally designed for rendering images and graphics, are highly parallel structures that are excellent for performing multiple tasks simultaneously. This makes them ideal for the complex computations required in robotics. Nvidia's GPUs became a key component in many robotic systems, providing the computational power necessary for tasks such as perception, navigation, and manipulation.

AI and Machine Learning

Nvidia's expertise in AI and machine learning also played a crucial role in its success in robotics. The company's AI platforms, like the Nvidia Jetson series, provided the brains for many autonomous robots. These platforms allowed robots to learn from their environments and adapt their behaviors accordingly, a capability that is fundamental to modern robotics.

Strategic Partnerships

In addition to its technological innovations, Nvidia also benefited from strategic partnerships with leading companies and research institutions in the robotics field. These collaborations allowed Nvidia to gain access to advanced robotics technologies and to influence the development of new systems and applications. For instance, its collaboration with Fanuc led to the integration of Nvidia's AI platform into Fanuc's manufacturing robots, demonstrating the practical applications of its technology in an industrial setting.

Understanding the Robotics Landscape

Lastly, Nvidia's success in robotics can be attributed to its understanding of the rapidly evolving landscape of AI and robotics. The company recognized early on the potential of robotics and made strategic decisions to position itself as a leader in this field. By focusing on the specific computational demands of robotics, Nvidia was able to provide solutions that were uniquely suited to this industry.

In conclusion, Nvidia's success in the robotics field was driven by a combination of innovative technologies, strategic partnerships, and a deep understanding of the robotics landscape. As the field of robotics continues to evolve, it is likely that Nvidia will continue to be at the forefront, shaping the future of this exciting industry.

CHAPTER 12: THE FUTURE OF ROBOTICS: NVIDIA'S VISION AND INNOVATIONS

In-depth look at the cutting-edge robotics technologies currently being developed by Nvidia

Nvidia is making significant strides in the world of robotics and AI. The company has developed a digital-twin robotics simulation application known as Isaac Sim. This tool allows researchers and developers to train and optimize AI in simulated industrial environments. Nvidia has introduced new sensor and lidar support to model real-world performance, a new conveyor-building tool, and a utility that adds people to the simulated environment.

One of the major challenges in training AI models for robotic applications is creating realistic, replicable work scenarios. For instance, work accidents are not always easy to recreate in real life, which presents a challenge for training AI. Isaac Sim addresses this issue by allowing developers to simulate these scenarios, enabling an industrial robot to react accordingly and perform its tasks correctly. For example, a robot that organizes and manages inventory must navigate heavily trafficked and changing areas, and Isaac Sim can help prepare the robot for these conditions.

In addition, Nvidia has been enhancing its mobile graphics processors, bringing its more efficient Ada Lovelace architecture to slim form factors. The introduction of GeForce RTX 40 Series Laptop GPUs represents what Nvidia describes as its largest generational leap for mobile graphics. These new GPUs provide significant speed-ups for 3-D, video, and broadcast workflows, plus additional AI tools that take advantage of ray tracing, AI, and video encoding hardware. They also support DLSS 3, AV1 encoding, and new Max-Q technologies that can fit into thinner, less power-hungry laptops. These enhancements are expected to benefit both gaming and content-creation demands, which remain high as hybrid work becomes more prevalent.

Nvidia is also improving its Omniverse and Studio offerings alongside these GPU upgrades. Omniverse, based on Universal Scene Description (USD), enables content creators to collaborate on various tools from makers such as Adobe and Autodesk. Nvidia has made the Blender alpha branch release available in the Omniverse launcher and announced performance updates to Audio2Face, Audio2Gesture, and Audio2Emotion. These powerful generative AI tools in Omniverse enable instant and realistic animation, allowing creators to automate certain tasks and focus on more challenging artistic endeavors.

Nvidia's innovations in robotics and AI demonstrate the company's commitment to advancing these fields and their potential applications in a variety of industries. The advancements in AI-powered graphics, mobile graphics processors, and collaborative content creation tools all contribute to a promising future for Nvidia in the realm of robotics and beyond.

Nvidia's Initial Robotics Research
Nvidia's foray into the field of robotics was driven by its vision of enabling next-generation robots to physically interact with

the environment and perform complex tasks alongside humans. This vision led to the establishment of the NVIDIA AI Robotics Research Lab in Seattle, a center of excellence that focuses on key areas such as robot manipulation, physics-based simulation, and robot perception. The lab's mission is to develop robust robots capable of interacting with the physical world and cooperating with humans in various industries including manufacturing, logistics, healthcare, and others.

Isaac Sim: Nvidia's Digital-Twin Robotics Simulation Application

To facilitate the development and optimization of AI in simulated industrial environments, Nvidia introduced Isaac Sim. This digital-twin robotics simulation application allows researchers and developers to train and optimize AI, mimicking real-world performance with the aid of new sensor and lidar support. One of the challenges in training an AI model for robotic applications is the replication of real-world work scenarios, such as a work accident, in the physical world. However, Isaac Sim's digital twin of the real world enables developers to train AI through unpredictable and volatile scenarios. This way, an industrial robot can learn to react appropriately to various situations and perform its duties accurately. For instance, a robot that organizes and manages inventory could be trained to navigate through heavily trafficked and changing areas.

A notable feature of Isaac Sim is its new people utility, which although currently offers a limited number of commands, holds significant potential for the future. It's envisioned that Nvidia will add support for environment-simulated behaviors, where developers can integrate a sample dataset of people's movements in different environments into Isaac Sim. This will provide the AI with more accurate data to learn from as compared to random or one-path movement.

Nvidia's Impact on Industrial Robotics

Industrial robots have been around for several decades, with their adoption often limited by factors like expense, setup time, and adaptability to changing environments. Nvidia's work in robotics has the potential to address these challenges, thereby revolutionizing the workplace. By optimizing AI training and operation using Isaac Sim, Nvidia and its partners could bring about significant changes in the way industrial robots are used, making them more versatile, efficient, and responsive to changing work scenarios.

Omniverse and Nvidia Drive Sim

In addition to Isaac Sim, Nvidia is also utilizing its Omniverse platform to design and plan state-of-the-art factories for vehicles. This is carried out in conjunction with Nvidia Drive Sim, a tool that helps in building software-defined vehicles. For instance, Mercedes-Benz announced that it is using Nvidia's Omniverse platform to design and plan its manufacturing and assembly facilities. The use of Nvidia Drive Sim and Omniverse allows Mercedes-Benz and other automotive manufacturers to design and produce vehicles in a digital-first process, ensuring minimal disruption to current operations while strategically laying out the production process.

Nvidia's initial foray into robotics demonstrates the company's commitment to enabling the next generation of robots and transforming industries with AI technology. Its research and development efforts are helping to overcome the challenges associated with traditional industrial robots and paving the way for more adaptable, efficient, and intelligent robotic systems.

Expert predictions and analysis of how Nvidia's work in robotics could shape the future of the industry

Given Nvidia's track record of innovation and influence in the technology sector, it's safe to say that its work in robotics will likely have a significant impact on the future of the industry. The company's strides in integrating AI and GPU technology into robotics have already begun to shape the way autonomous systems are designed and used, and it's expected that this trend will continue.

Integration of AI in Robotics

One of the key aspects that experts are paying attention to is the integration of AI in robotics. Nvidia has been at the forefront of this trend, using its AI platforms like the Jetson series to make robots more autonomous and capable of learning from their environments. As AI continues to advance, robots equipped with these technologies are expected to become more versatile and able to handle a wider range of tasks. This could potentially revolutionize industries such as manufacturing, logistics, healthcare, and more.

Edge Computing

Another area where Nvidia's work could shape the future of robotics is in edge computing. With the advent of the Internet of Things (IoT) and the increasing need for real-time processing in robotics, edge computing is becoming more critical. Nvidia's GPUs and AI platforms are well-suited to this task, as they can process large amounts of data quickly and locally, reducing the need for constant communication with a central server. This could lead to more efficient and responsive robotic systems.

Collaborations and Partnerships

Nvidia's collaborations and partnerships with other leading companies and research institutions in the field of robotics are also expected to influence the industry's future. Through these partnerships, Nvidia is able to access and contribute to cutting-edge research and development, helping to drive innovation in the field.

Educational Impact

Nvidia's educational initiatives in AI and robotics are also shaping the future of the industry. By providing resources and platforms for learning, such as the Deep Learning Institute, Nvidia is helping to train the next generation of engineers and scientists who will continue to push the boundaries of what is possible in robotics.

In conclusion, Nvidia's work in robotics is poised to have a significant impact on the future of the industry. Through its technological innovations, partnerships, and educational initiatives, Nvidia is not only shaping the capabilities of current robotic systems, but also influencing the direction of future developments in the field.

CHAPTER 13: THE NVIDIA STOCK PHENOMENON

In-depth analysis of Nvidia's stock performance, with exploration of the driving factors behind its growth

Nvidia, a renowned player in the technology sector, is well recognized for its graphics processing units (GPUs) which are widely used in both the gaming industry and professional markets. Additionally, Nvidia's products have been pivotal in the Artificial Intelligence (AI) field, data centers, and autonomous driving technology.

As of my last update in September 2021, Nvidia's stock performance was robust, largely due to its leadership in the graphics card industry and its strategic expansion into high-growth markets like AI and data centers. The advent of AI and machine learning technologies led to a surge in demand for Nvidia's GPUs, which are used to train these complex models.

Nvidia's financial performance in the fiscal year 2023 was flat compared to the previous year, with a total revenue of $27.0 billion. However, the Q4 revenue of $6.05 billion was down 21% from a year ago. The GAAP earnings per diluted share for the fiscal year 2023 were $1.74, down 55% from a year ago, while Non-GAAP earnings per diluted share were $3.34, down 25% from a year ago. Notably, there was a return to shareholders of $1.15 billion in Q4 and $10.44 billion in the fiscal year.

Despite the downturn in Q4, Nvidia's CEO, Jensen Huang, highlighted the company's optimism for the future, indicating an inflection point in AI with broad adoption expected across various industries. There is an accelerated interest in generative AI, and Nvidia is gearing up to take advantage of these developments through their AI supercomputer, acceleration libraries software, and pretrained generative AI models. The gaming segment is also recovering from the post-pandemic downturn, with gamers enthusiastically embracing Nvidia's new Ada architecture GPUs with AI neural rendering.

Looking ahead, Nvidia's outlook for the first quarter of fiscal 2024 projects a revenue of $6.50 billion, plus or minus 2%, with GAAP and non-GAAP gross margins expected to be 64.1% and 66.5%, respectively.

*Examination of the company's
financial prospects, with
insights from financial analysts
and industry experts*

NVIDIA's financial performance in the fourth quarter and fiscal year 2023 showed both strengths and challenges. Here are some highlights:

Revenue: NVIDIA's Q4 FY23 revenue was $6.05 billion, down 21% from a year ago but up 2% from the previous quarter. The fiscal year 2023 revenue was flat at $26.97 billion.

Earnings: The GAAP earnings per diluted share for Q4 FY23 were $0.57, down 52% from a year ago but up 111% from the previous quarter. For fiscal 2023, GAAP earnings per diluted share were $1.74, down 55% from a year ago. Non-GAAP earnings per diluted share were $0.88 for Q4 FY23 and $3.34 for fiscal 2023, marking a decrease from the previous year.

Shareholder Returns: During Q4 FY23, NVIDIA returned to shareholders $1.15 billion in share repurchases and cash dividends, bringing the return in the fiscal year to $10.44 billion. NVIDIA will pay its next quarterly cash dividend of $0.04 per share on March 29, 2023.

Company Outlook: For the first quarter of fiscal 2024, NVIDIA expects revenue to be $6.50 billion, GAAP and non-GAAP gross margins to be 64.1% and 66.5% respectively, and GAAP and non-GAAP operating expenses to be approximately $2.53 billion and $1.78 billion respectively.

Regarding NVIDIA's strategic direction and future prospects:

The company is focusing on the adoption of artificial intelligence (AI), particularly in the field of generative AI. NVIDIA's CEO, Jensen Huang, noted that the company is positioned to help customers take advantage of breakthroughs in generative AI and large language models through its new AI supercomputer, which is in full production.

NVIDIA is also partnering with leading cloud service providers to offer AI-as-a-service. This offering will give enterprises access to NVIDIA's AI platform, including its AI supercomputer, acceleration libraries software, and pretrained generative AI models, as a cloud service. NVIDIA's DGX AI supercomputer is already offered on Oracle Cloud Infrastructure, with other platforms like Microsoft Azure and Google Cloud Platform expected soon.

CHAPTER 14:
THE FINANCIAL
RIPPLE EFFECT

*Detailed discussion of Nvidia's
financial success and its wider
implications for the tech
industry and the economy*

As of 2021, Nvidia had established itself as a leader in the tech industry, particularly in the field of artificial intelligence (AI). The company's success is largely driven by its pioneering work in graphics processing units (GPUs), which are integral to AI technologies. Its GPUs are utilized in a wide range of applications, from gaming and professional visualization to data centers and automotive AI systems. The company's innovative approach to AI has made it a key player in the industry.

In recent news, Nvidia's stock surged by 24% after its stellar revenue forecast, highlighting the transformative potential of AI. This surge increased the company's market capitalization significantly, making it twice as big as the second-largest chip firm, Taiwan's TSMC, and the fifth-most valuable U.S. company. This success has had broader implications for the tech industry, sparking a rally in the chip sector and AI-focused firms and elevating stock markets globally. Nvidia's position in the AI chip market suggests that its financial success is likely to continue as

AI technologies continue to evolve and expand.

Furthermore, Nvidia's innovative AI research and product offerings, such as generative AI models and AI-powered visual tools, have contributed to its financial success and have broad implications for various industries. From transforming text into images to creating lifelike 3D characters, Nvidia's technologies are pushing the boundaries of what's possible in areas such as film, game development, and even autonomous vehicle training.

In the wider context, Nvidia's financial success serves as a testament to the economic potential of AI technologies. As AI continues to revolutionize industries across the globe, companies leading the way, like Nvidia, stand to reap significant financial rewards. Furthermore, Nvidia's growth and innovation in AI suggest that the tech industry, and indeed the global economy, is increasingly reliant on the development and application of AI technologies.

Analysis of Jensen Huang's growing wealth and influence, and what this indicates about the state of the tech industry

Jensen Huang, the co-founder and CEO of NVIDIA, has seen his wealth and influence grow significantly in recent years, mirroring the growth of his company and its place in the tech industry. NVIDIA, under Huang's leadership, has risen to prominence as a major player in the tech industry, particularly in the field of artificial intelligence (AI) and graphics processing units (GPUs). This article will examine Huang's growing wealth and influence and what it indicates about the broader tech industry.

Wealth and Influence

Huang's wealth has soared as NVIDIA's stock price has risen due to the company's successful expansion into various high-growth tech sectors. NVIDIA originally focused on GPUs for gaming, but it has successfully pivoted to leverage its technology for more diverse applications, such as AI, autonomous vehicles, and data centers. This strategic shift has not only bolstered NVIDIA's financial performance but also significantly increased Huang's net worth, given his substantial shareholding in the company.

Huang's influence extends beyond his wealth. As the CEO of one of the leading tech companies, his views and decisions have a significant impact on the industry. His strategic foresight in recognizing the potential of GPUs for AI and other applications has been instrumental in shaping NVIDIA's direction and, by extension, influencing trends in the tech sector. His advocacy for AI and advanced GPU technology has encouraged other companies to explore these areas, reinforcing the significance of these technologies in the industry.

State of the Tech Industry

The growth of Huang's wealth and influence is indicative of several broader trends in the tech industry:

AI and Machine Learning: Huang's focus on AI reflects the tech industry's growing emphasis on these technologies. AI and machine learning are transforming many industries, from healthcare to finance to entertainment. NVIDIA's success in this area underscores the increasing value and influence of companies that can offer cutting-edge AI technologies and solutions.

High-Performance Computing: NVIDIA's expertise in GPUs has positioned it at the forefront of the high-performance computing sector. This technology is crucial for supporting AI, machine learning, and advanced analytics, which are increasingly important in the tech industry and beyond.

Cloud Computing: Huang's push into offering NVIDIA's AI platform as a cloud service aligns with the tech industry's rapid shift toward cloud computing. The ability to offer powerful computing capabilities as a service has become a key competitive advantage in the tech industry.

Leadership and Vision: Finally, Huang's growing influence underscores the importance of strong leadership and a clear strategic vision in the tech industry. His ability to navigate NVIDIA through technological shifts and new market opportunities has been a critical factor in the company's success.

In conclusion, Jensen Huang's increasing wealth and influence reflect NVIDIA's strategic success in key growth areas of the tech industry, including AI, high-performance computing, and cloud services. His leadership and vision for NVIDIA highlight the importance of these factors in driving a company's – and an individual's – success in the tech industry.

CHAPTER 15: THE ROAD AHEAD: NVIDIA'S FUTURE IN AI

Analysis of Nvidia's potential future role in the AI industry

Nvidia has positioned itself as a significant player in the AI industry, with various strategic moves indicating their commitment to this sector. In the recent years, the company has introduced a range of advanced AI hardware and software solutions, and is partnering with leading cloud service providers to offer AI-as-a-service. This includes providing enterprises access to Nvidia's world-leading AI platform through the Nvidia AI Cloud Service Offerings, which allows users to engage with Nvidia's AI supercomputer, acceleration libraries software, or pretrained generative AI models as a cloud service. The Nvidia DGX™ AI supercomputer is already offered on Oracle Cloud Infrastructure, with Microsoft Azure, Google Cloud Platform and others expected to join soon. At the AI platform software layer, customers can access Nvidia AI Enterprise for training and deploying large language models or other AI workloads. Nvidia also offers its NeMo™ and BioNeMo™ customizable AI models to enterprise customers who want to build proprietary generative AI models and services for their businesses.

The company's CEO, Jensen Huang, believes that AI is at an

inflection point for broad adoption across various industries. Nvidia is poised to help customers leverage the capabilities of generative AI and large language models with its new AI supercomputer, which features the H100 and its Transformer Engine and Quantum-2 networking fabric. Gaming is also seeing a recovery from the post-pandemic downturn, with gamers enthusiastically embracing the new Ada architecture GPUs with AI neural rendering.

However, Nvidia's financial performance has been mixed. In Q4 of fiscal 2023, the company reported a quarterly revenue of $6.05 billion, which was down 21% from a year ago but up 2% from the previous quarter. The fiscal year revenue was $26.97 billion, flat from a year ago. There were significant drops in net income and diluted earnings per share compared to the previous year, but there were also notable increases from the previous quarter. Despite the mixed financial performance, the company returned significant amounts to its shareholders: $1.15 billion in the fourth quarter and $10.44 billion over the fiscal year.

Looking ahead to the first quarter of fiscal 2024, Nvidia expects a revenue of $6.50 billion, with both GAAP and non-GAAP gross margins expected to be 64.1% and 66.5%, respectively. Operating expenses are projected to be approximately $2.53 billion and $1.78 billion for GAAP and non-GAAP, respectively. The tax rates are expected to be around 13.0%.

*Insights into Jensen Huang's
vision for the future of AI
and Nvidia's place in it*

Jensen Huang, CEO of Nvidia, has a highly optimistic vision for the future of AI and the role of Nvidia in this rapidly evolving field. Huang predicts a trillion-dollar shift towards accelerated computing as generative AI becomes integral to every product, service, and business process. This belief is supported by the recent surge in demand for Nvidia's products and services.

Nvidia's recent stock surge of 24% in a single day has been driven by its strong revenue forecast and the general belief that Wall Street is yet to fully price in the transformative potential of AI. This surge has more than doubled Nvidia's stock value for the year and raised the chip designer's market capitalization to nearly $939 billion, making it twice as large as the second-largest chip firm, Taiwan's TSMC2. Nvidia's future revenue is expected to be significantly above the average Wall Street estimate, and the company is preparing to meet a surge in demand for AI chips in the second half of the year.

Under Huang's leadership, Nvidia is significantly investing in AI research and development. This has resulted in a plethora of new AI models and techniques that are transforming the way creators and developers work, as showcased in their 20 research papers headed to SIGGRAPH 2023. For example, Nvidia's generative AI models can now transform text into personalized images in just a few seconds, providing a powerful tool for creators. New techniques also allow for the automatic transformation of 2D images and videos into 3D representations, bringing lifelike motion to 3D characters, simulating complex hair dynamics in real-time, and generating photorealistic visuals in real-time for video games and digital twins.

The future implications of these chip advancements and the launch of Eos supercomputer

The advancements in chip technology announced in 2023, including the H100 GPU and the Grace CPU Superchip, indicate a promising future for Nvidia in the AI industry. These developments will likely play a crucial role in determining Nvidia's future direction and its potential influence in the rapidly evolving AI landscape.

The H100 GPU and Grace CPU Superchip's ability to significantly reduce AI processing times from weeks to days could have profound implications for numerous industries. These chips could facilitate faster development and deployment of AI applications across diverse fields, ranging from entertainment to healthcare. They also reaffirm Nvidia's commitment to advancing AI technology and its position as a leader in the industry.

The implications of these advancements extend beyond Nvidia's hardware. The introduction of these chips could accelerate the adoption of AI technology by making it more accessible and efficient. This, in turn, could stimulate innovation and growth in the broader tech industry.

The launch of the Eos supercomputer, which Nvidia claims will be the world's fastest AI system, is another indication of the company's ambitious vision for the future of AI. Eos has the potential to redefine the boundaries of AI capabilities, potentially opening up new possibilities for AI applications in areas such as scientific research, climate modeling, and healthcare.

These advancements also underscore the growing competition in the AI infrastructure market, particularly between Nvidia and other tech giants like Intel and AMD. The introduction of the H100 GPU and the Grace CPU Superchip, as well as the launch of Eos, will likely intensify this competition, influencing the future trajectory of the AI industry.

As Nvidia continues to innovate, its future in AI appears bright. The advancements announced in 2023 have reinforced the company's role as a key player in the AI industry, and they are likely to shape the future of AI technology in the years to come.

Nvidia's continued focus on AI development, as seen in its 2023 advancements

Nvidia's continued dedication to pushing the boundaries of AI technology was further exemplified in 2023, with the unveiling of the H100 GPU, the Grace CPU Superchip, and the Eos supercomputer. These advancements reflect Nvidia's unwavering commitment to AI development and underscore its role as an industry leader.

The H100 GPU and Grace CPU Superchip are not merely new products; they are testament to Nvidia's enduring focus on improving AI's computational efficiency and performance. By significantly reducing AI processing times, these chips have the potential to transform AI application development and deployment across various industries. Their introduction reaffirms Nvidia's position at the forefront of AI technology innovation.

The Eos supercomputer, anticipated to be the world's fastest AI system upon operation, symbolizes Nvidia's ongoing ambition to redefine the capabilities of AI. With potential applications in scientific research, climate modeling, and healthcare, Eos could stimulate a new wave of innovation in AI technology.

These advancements demonstrate Nvidia's strategic focus on maintaining and expanding its influence in the AI industry. They also highlight the company's dedication to fostering innovation, driving technological progress, and supporting the broader adoption and application of AI.

In light of these developments, Nvidia's future role in AI seems promising. As the company continues to pioneer new advancements and push the boundaries of what's possible in AI, it reinforces its position as a key player in shaping the future of AI technology.

The potential influence of Nvidia's advancements in healthcare, automotive, and other sectors

The advancements that Nvidia has made in AI technology, particularly with the introduction of the H100 GPU, the Grace CPU Superchip, and the Eos supercomputer, have far-reaching implications across multiple sectors, including healthcare and automotive.

In healthcare, Nvidia's AI capabilities have been harnessed to develop solutions that can predict patient readmission rates. In collaboration with NYU Langone Health, Nvidia developed NYUTron, a large language model that is helping doctors identify patients who might be at a higher risk of readmission. Such predictive tools are not only enhancing healthcare efficiency but also improving patient outcomes. The model has so far been applied to more than 50,000 patients, and it has the potential to be adopted by other healthcare institutions, indicating a future where AI-driven diagnostics and predictive care become the norm.

In the automotive sector, Nvidia is making strides in autonomous vehicle technology. Its autonomous vehicle computer, Drive Orin, began shipping in 2023 and has been adopted by electric vehicle makers such as BYD Co Ltd and Lucid Motors for their next-generation fleets. Nvidia's CFO, Colette Kress, noted that software for the automotive market will be a key driver for the company, highlighting the growing importance of AI in this sector. Nvidia's vice president for automotive, Danny Shapiro, estimated that there was $11 billion worth of automotive business in the pipeline over the next six years, with revenue coming from both hardware and increased, recurring revenue from Nvidia software.

Beyond healthcare and automotive, Nvidia's advancements have the potential to revolutionize other sectors, from climate modeling to scientific research and beyond. With AI-powered supercomputers like Eos, industries can process vast amounts of data at unprecedented speeds, unlocking new possibilities for discovery and innovation. As Nvidia continues to innovate and push the boundaries of AI technology, it is set to drive transformative changes across various sectors, further solidifying its pivotal role in the AI revolution.

CONCLUSION

Nvidia's journey, from its inception to its current standing as a leading force in the AI and robotics industry, is nothing short of inspiring. Under the visionary leadership of Jensen Huang, the company has navigated numerous challenges and seized opportunities, resulting in transformative technological innovations.

The company's advancements in AI chips, GPU technology, and their applications in various fields, including robotics, have redefined the technological landscape. Nvidia's efforts have not only revolutionized the capabilities of AI and robotics but have also sparked a broader shift towards more intelligent and autonomous systems in various sectors of society.

The company's financial success and the ripple effects it has created in the tech industry and economy as a whole underscore the far-reaching implications of its work. From investors to developers and end-users, many have felt the impact of Nvidia's relentless pursuit of innovation.

Looking ahead, Nvidia's potential in the rapidly evolving AI and robotics industry appears vast. With its strong foundation, continuous investment in research and development, strategic collaborations, and commitment to education and community building, Nvidia is well-positioned to drive and shape the future of these fields.

However, as we reflect on Nvidia's success, it's also important to recognize that the road ahead is likely to be filled with unknowns. New technological breakthroughs, regulatory changes, and shifts in societal needs and attitudes could all influence Nvidia's trajectory in ways that are difficult to predict.

Nevertheless, if the past is any indication, Nvidia, under the leadership of Jensen Huang, will likely continue to be at the forefront of technological progress, playing a crucial role in shaping the future of AI and robotics. Through its work, Nvidia is processing the mind of artificial intelligence, thereby pushing the boundaries of what's possible and redefining our relationship with technology.

Reflection on Nvidia's journey, its transformative impact on AI, and its influence on the tech industry

NVIDIA's journey over the years has been a remarkable one, marked by innovation, adaptability, and a transformative impact on artificial intelligence (AI) and the broader tech industry.

Founded in 1993 as a graphics processing unit (GPU) manufacturer, NVIDIA initially focused on the gaming market. The company made a name for itself with its high-performance GPUs, which were critical for rendering complex graphics in video games. Over the years, NVIDIA's graphics technology became the gold standard in the gaming industry.

However, the company's true transformative journey began when it recognized the potential of GPUs beyond gaming. Under the leadership of Jensen Huang, NVIDIA pioneered the use of GPUs for parallel computing. This opened up new markets for the company, particularly in scientific computing and AI.

NVIDIA's GPUs became the backbone of many AI applications due to their ability to efficiently process large amounts of data simultaneously. This capability made them ideal for training deep learning models, which require massive computational power. NVIDIA capitalized on this opportunity by developing CUDA, a proprietary programming language that allows developers to use their GPUs for general-purpose computing.

The company's transformative impact on AI has been profound. Its technology has accelerated the development and deployment of AI, enabling advancements in fields ranging from healthcare to autonomous vehicles. NVIDIA's AI platform has become a critical tool for researchers, developers, and businesses, driving innovation and progress in AI.

NVIDIA's influence on the tech industry is also significant. By demonstrating the potential of GPUs for diverse applications, NVIDIA has inspired other tech companies to explore similar paths. This has led to the emergence of new markets and opportunities, stimulating innovation and competition in the tech industry.

Moreover, NVIDIA's foray into AI-as-a-service represents a major trend in the tech industry: the shift towards cloud computing. By offering its AI platform as a cloud service, NVIDIA is making its cutting-edge technology more accessible to businesses and developers, fueling the democratization of AI.

In conclusion, NVIDIA's journey is a testament to the power of innovation, strategic foresight, and adaptability. Its transformative impact on AI and the tech industry underscores the company's role as a trailblazer, setting trends and opening new possibilities. As we look to the future, NVIDIA is well-positioned to continue driving progress in AI and shaping the tech industry.

Summary of Jensen Huang's visionary leadership and its role in Nvidia's success

Jensen Huang, as the CEO of Nvidia, has been instrumental in driving the company's success, primarily by recognizing the transformative potential of artificial intelligence (AI) and positioning Nvidia as a leading player in this field. His visionary leadership foresaw the pervasive integration of generative AI into every product, service, and business process, leading to a predicted trillion-dollar shift towards accelerated computing.

Huang's forward-thinking approach, combined with Nvidia's strong revenue forecast, has resulted in significant financial success. A recent surge in Nvidia's stock value, driven by the belief that the transformative potential of AI has yet to be fully priced in by Wall Street, doubled the company's value for the year and raised its market capitalization to nearly $939 billion.

Under Huang's leadership, Nvidia has made substantial investments in AI research and development, producing cutting-edge technologies that are revolutionizing industries. The company's research, highlighted in their 20 papers headed to SIGGRAPH 2023, showcases a host of new AI models and techniques. These advancements include generative AI models capable of converting text into personalized images rapidly, techniques to automatically transform 2D images and videos into 3D representations, AI systems that impart lifelike motion to 3D characters, methods for simulating complex hair dynamics in real-time, and the generation of photorealistic visuals in real-time for video games and digital twins.

In summary, Jensen Huang's visionary leadership and strategic focus on AI has been a key factor in Nvidia's success. By recognizing the game-changing potential of AI and directing Nvidia's resources towards the development of innovative AI technologies, Huang has positioned Nvidia at the forefront of the AI revolution, leading to significant financial gains and transformative technological advancements.

Final thoughts on the potential implications and opportunities for Nvidia in the rapidly evolving AI landscape.

As we step further into the AI era, Nvidia's role as a leading innovator becomes increasingly crucial. The company's groundbreaking work in AI chips, coupled with its expanding research in generative AI, underlines its unwavering commitment to advancing the field.

As AI continues to permeate every facet of life, Nvidia's strategic position in this landscape is likely to generate immense opportunities. Its foundational work in AI chips and high-performance computing has placed it at the epicenter of AI's expansion, with applications ranging from data centers to autonomous vehicles, healthcare, gaming, and beyond. Moreover, the company's forays into generative AI and its close collaborations with leading AI organizations place it at the cutting edge of AI's future innovations.

The implications of this are vast. For one, as more sectors turn to AI for solutions, Nvidia's chips and AI technologies will likely see increasing demand. As Nvidia CEO Jensen Huang has predicted, a trillion-dollar shift towards accelerated computing is anticipated as generative AI becomes a staple in every product, service, and business process. This presents a substantial opportunity for Nvidia to continue its upward trajectory and solidify its status as a leader in the AI industry.

Moreover, as AI progresses and becomes more complex, new challenges will arise. Nvidia's ongoing research and development efforts, particularly in generative AI and neural graphics, are poised to address these challenges, providing solutions that could revolutionize industries and redefine the bounds of what's possible with AI.

In summary, the rapidly evolving AI landscape presents exciting opportunities for Nvidia. Under the visionary leadership of Jensen Huang, Nvidia is expected to continue to play a leading role in AI's development, contributing to revolutionary breakthroughs and shaping the future of technology.

Addendum

The realm of robotics continues to evolve at an unprecedented pace, and as such, Nvidia's role in this field is subject to rapid changes and developments. It's essential to note that the company's influence in robotics is not limited to the areas outlined above.

Nvidia's advancements in GPU technology and AI continue to redefine what's possible in robotics. The company's ongoing research and development efforts are likely to yield even more groundbreaking technologies and applications that will further transform the industry.

Moreover, Nvidia's commitment to fostering a vibrant ecosystem around its technologies—through developer resources, open-source contributions, and other initiatives—is an integral part of its impact on the field of robotics. By empowering others to build upon its technologies, Nvidia is catalyzing innovation and accelerating the progress of robotics at large.

Finally, while this analysis offers an overview of Nvidia's influence on the robotics industry, it's important to remember that the field is influenced by a multitude of factors, including regulatory environments, economic conditions, and societal needs and attitudes. As such, the future of robotics will be shaped not only by technological advancements but also by how these technologies are adopted and applied across various sectors of society.

☆☆☆☆☆